thegoodwebguide

genealogy

www.thegoodwebguide.co.uk

Dedication

This book is dedicated, with love and thanks, to my husband Jonathan, whose mother once fondly described him as a 'family history bore'. He, and earlier my father, Hubert Dingwall, have actually proved to me that tracing one's family history is by no means boring.

thegoodwebguide

genealogy

Caroline Peacock

The Good Web Guide Limited • London

First Published in Great Britain in 2000 by The Good Web Guide Limited
Broadwall House, 21 Broadwall, London, SE1 9PL

www.thegoodwebguide.co.uk

Email:feedback@thegoodwebguide.co.uk

© 2000 The Good Web Guide Ltd

Text © 2000 Caroline Peacock

Original series concept by Steve Bailey.

Cover photo © The Image Bank

10 9 8 7 6 5 4 3 2

A catalogue record for this book is available from the British Library.

ISBN 1-903282-06-3

The publishers and author have done their best to ensure the accuracy and
currency of all information in this volume, however they can accept no
responsibility for any loss or inconvenience sustained by any reader as a
result of its information or advice.

Project Editor Michelle Clare

Design by Myriad Creative Ltd

Printed in Italy at LEGO S.p.A.

user key

£	Subscription		IT	Italy
R	Registration Required		JA	Jamaica
🔒	Secure Online Ordering		JE	Jewish
			NE	Netherlands

key to countries

AUS	Australia		NZ	New Zealand
CAN	Canada		SA	South Africa
EUR	Europe		SW	Switzerland
G	Germany		UK	United Kingdom
IRE	Ireland		US	United States
IS	Israel		WI	West Indies

contents

the good web guides

The World Wide Web is a vast resource, with millions of sites on every conceivable subject. There are people who have made it their mission to surf the net: cyber-communities have grown, and people have formed relationships and even married on the net.

However, the reality for most people is that they don't have the time or inclination to surf the net for hours on end. Busy people want to use the internet for quick access to information. You don't have to spend hours on the internet looking for answers to your questions and you don't have to be an accomplished net surfer or cyber wizard to get the most out of the web. It can be a quick and useful resource if you are looking for specific information.

The Good Web Guides have been published with this in mind. To give you a head start in your search, our researchers have looked at hundreds of sites and what you will find in the Good Web Guides is a collection of reviews of the best we've found.

The Good Web Guide recommendation is impartial and all the sites have been visited several times. Reviews are focused on the website and what it sets out to do, rather than an endorsement of a company, or their product. A small but beautiful site run by a one-man band may be rated higher than an ambitious but flawed site run by a mighty organisation.

Relevance to the UK-based visitor is also given a high premium: tantalising as it is to read about purchases you can make in California, because of delivery charges, import duties and controls it may not be as useful as a local site.

Our reviewers considered a number of questions when reviewing the sites, such as: How quickly do the sites and individual pages download? Can you move around the site easily and get back to where you started, and do the links work? Is the information up to date and accurate? And is the site pleasing to the eye and easy to read? More importantly, we also asked whether the site has something distinctive to offer, whether it be entertainment, inspiration or pure information. On the basis of the answers to these questions sites are given ratings out of five. As we aim only to include sites that we feel are of serious interest, there are very few low-rated sites.

Bear in mind that the collection of reviews you see here are just a snapshot of the sites at a particular time. The process of choosing and writing about sites is rather like painting the Forth Bridge: as each section appears complete, new sites are launched and others are modified. When you've registered at the Good Web Guide site (see p.159 for further details) you can check out the reviews of new sites and updates of existing ones, or even have them emailed to you. By using the cd rom at the back of the book or registering at our site, you'll find hot links to all the sites listed, so you can just click and go without needing to type the addresses accurately into your browser.

As this is the first edition of the Good Web Guide, all our sites have been reviewed by the author and research team, but we'd like to know what you think. Contact us via the website or email feedback@thegoodwebguide.co.uk. You are welcome to recommend sites, quibble about the ratings, point out changes and inaccuracies or suggest new features to assess.

You can find us at www.thegoodwebguide.co.uk

introduction

This book has been exciting to write, exciting as part of the Good Web Guide's overall plan, and exciting as a personal project. For some time, a guide to the worldwide genealogy resources of the internet, aimed at helping UK-based researchers, has been badly needed. There are several, good, meaty books out there explaining how to tackle online research into family history from the North American viewpoint, but until now, there hasn't been one written from the UK perspective. I am grateful to the Good Web Guides for giving me the opportunity to create that book.

It is true that there are some brief booklets, some of them listed here, which direct UK-based researchers to useful genealogical websites, and I acknowledge them with gratitude. But it has been a thrilling quest to explore the vast, unruly resources of the internet and try to sift out the very best genealogy websites, both British and international, for the benefit of UK users.

I have visited many, many more websites than I have reviewed here, and I have made a serious attempt to select the best and explain why they are the best. If your favourite website isn't here, don't fume in silence, please. I would love to know about it, have a look at it, and perhaps include it in one of the regular updates that the Good Web Guides plan to produce in future months. Websites on the internet move, alter, expand and collapse with alarming regularity, so the opportunity to provide online updates is a brilliant idea and a vital new service. You will find the Good Web Guide's email address listed at the end of this introduction, so please don't be shy about using it!

The many hours spent online have been fascinating, rewarding and, at times, exasperating. I have found that there are still, as yet, relatively few sites where the family historian can search so-called primary data online. Perhaps, in fact, this is the moment to decide, once and for all, what counts as primary data, what is secondary and what, in my terminology, is tertiary.

There is, in fact, no primary data on the Internet. Primary data, strictly speaking, is original documents, such as the actual Parish Record hand-written by a parish priest. Some such records, most notably those in the famous IGI (International Genealogical Index), have been transcribed onto microfiches and, more recently, into an online form on the Internet, but wherever transcription is involved a possibility of inaccuracy creeps in. Misreadings of old-fashioned handwriting is only one problem. Actual mischief becomes a possibility, as is illustrated by one now celebrated case in the 1881 Census record. In this instance, a family appears whose members lived to impossibly advanced ages, fathered children either in their infancy or in their dotage (or indeed even before they were themselves born) and employed improbable servants from countries all over the globe. This is now recognised as an elaborate joke, but it explains why transcribed data has to be considered 'secondary' data.

Another example, from my own experience, makes a similar point. I recently had cause to consult the complete works of John Ruskin, which run to more than 30 volumes. To get them transcribed as accurately as possible, the Ruskin Archive had employed three secretaries, each of whom typed their way through the whole lot. The three transcriptions were then superimposed, so as to flag up any possible inaccuracies, and any failures of identicality were individually checked. This is the sort of procedural excellence that top-quality transcription requires. And even

then, it still has to be termed 'secondary' data.

At the next level are family histories compiled by individuals, and these, though often loosely termed secondary material, are, in my view, tertiary records. It is essential that the novice family historian should treat these with extreme care. When a little bit of a gap opens up in the family tree and absolute certainty can't be assured, it may become all too tempting to take just a tiny leap of faith and 'adopt' an ancestor as part of the tree without being 100 per cent sure that the link is correctly made.

Some, perhaps most, family historians are extremely rigorous about checking their sources. A few are not. So, if you approach a general namesearch website, and there are plenty to attract you with several good ones being listed here, do so with extreme caution. If you find yourself offered a family tree in a one-name website or by means of a personal GEDCOM (GEnealogical Data COMmunication) file, don't necessarily accept it all as gospel. The mantra of the really dedicated genealogist is 'Check, check and check again'.

Please may I urge you to be particularly cautious when you are offered all sorts of not inexpensive gifts, even from bodies so apparently reputable as Burke's Peerage. Keep your discriminating wits about you and check very carefully before you are seduced into thinking that you belong to a noble line, are entitled to bear arms and should accordingly commission an inscribed pedigree complete with ancient seal — let alone have your family crest printed on wall-plaques, mugs and T-shirts!

These caveats aside, there are great, great genealogical and family history riches to be explored on the internet. All the web sites I know of that allow you to consult actual transcribed records are here. So are all those, and these are in the majority, that tell you where vital records are to be found. In addition, there is also a host of enthralling websites where simply trawling around, and following up slender threads, may lead to wonderful discoveries.

If we're being fussy about terminology, a genealogist is one who is seeking to trace his or her family tree back generation by generation, deviating neither to left nor right. A family historian, on the other hand, is captivated by the wider picture and moves out, laterally, to explore the historical or social context in which his or her ancestors lived. Both are entirely honourable pursuits and I confess that, for the sake of brevity, I have used the term 'genealogist' rather than 'family history researcher' within the website reviews that follow. My apologies if this offends any purists.

A few other words of explanation may be useful here. When I say 'on the occasion tested... ' it usually means that I have taken a family name or other reference that I know should produce a particular result, in order to see whether the outcome is satisfactory.

I have had to make some painful exclusions from the list. It was immediately clear that there would not be room to include a list of one-name websites, especially as new ones are being posted daily, but that I could only mention the umbrella organisations through which you can find out about them. In due course, it also became plain that individual local Family History Societies and even good local records centres, like the admirable Borthwick Institute of Historical Research in York, would have to be left out too. For the same reason local and university libraries are not listed here either. I can confidently assure you, however, that the links to all of these are to be found from within other websites reviewed here.

That leads me to another problem, that of overlap. There are many websites that cover a huge amount of ground. Some not only provide basic guidance, list data resources and give details of access, but also offer online tutorials, list coming events, sell books online and link to namesearch facilities. Deciding where to categorise them has been difficult. In the end I have sought to situate each one in the most comfortably applicable chapter as a main entry and then refer to it again under other headings with cross-references. I hope this makes the book as user-friendly as possible.

I would quite have liked to have listed sites that are not worth bothering with, too! A good example, I'm sorry to say, would have been www.Churchnet.org.uk. When tested, it informed me that there is apparently no church at all in the parish where I live and clicking on the encouraging button 'genealogies' only brought up a page saying, admittedly apologetically, that they have neither the time nor the resources to help. The 'Searches' message board looked more promising, I thought, until I found that it lists all those dozens of requests posted so far, sorted only by date of posting, not by name or even locality; useless.

Finally, I have tended to exclude obviously illiterate sites, such as the one in which the words 'granfather', 'hundreth' and 'ficticious' (sic) all appear in a single, quite brief homepage, though I acknowledge that this may be more the fault of the website designer than its owner. A bad homepage is off-putting, nevertheless. Web designers and owners, take note!

Well, as I promised, here's how to get back at me if you don't like (or perhaps if you do) what you find here. I'm learning, too, and I will be very glad indeed to hear from you.

Caroline Peacock, July 2000

Email address: info@thegoodwebguide.com

Chapter 1

genealogy and the web

Ancestral research on the web

The purpose of this book is to help those who are interested either in tracing the descents of their families from ancestors to the present day (genealogy) or in building a wider picture of those people's lives (family history), by making use of the internet for the first time. Many researchers want, in fact, to build up a composite picture, taking the route of both the genealogist and the family historian. Some will already have done quite a lot of research and will be seeking merely to consolidate and extend it with reference to the web. Others will be tackling the subject for the first time.

Can I do it all on the web?

The first question many researchers ask is, 'Can I do it all on the web?' It is certainly true that there is a lot of information, both genealogical and historical, now available on the web and it is being added to all the time, but the short answer to that question has to be 'No'. Unfortunately, it is not possible, or certainly not yet, to start from scratch and build up a complete family tree using just a PC and a modem.

There are two reasons why this is so. One, as explained in the Introduction, is that there are still very few actual records available for consultation online. Much the biggest, fully searchable, online record is without question the famous International Genealogical Index (IGI), which is still being compiled by the members of the Church of Jesus Christ of the Latter-Day Saints. (It can, of course, also be consulted in microfiche form in county and some local libraries, as well as in Family History centres run by the Church).

The 1901 Census is in the process of being digitised for eventual release on the web, but no Census records can currently be consulted online. The 1881 Census, however, is available in its entirety on CD-ROM and the 1851 Census is partially available by the same means; copies of these can be ordered online. The first Census was taken in 1801 and all Census records, taken every ten years, are lodged at the Family Records Centre in London. Things are changing fast, however, and it is clear that in a few years' time many more records will be searchable online and the situation will be completely transformed. Even when much larger bodies of data are transcribed, however, researchers using the web will do well to remember that they will still be consulting secondary records (records that have been transcribed) rather than the original, primary documents.

The second reason why it is not possible to do all family history research on the web is that even such material as is available doesn't come close enough to the present day. You will still need to start by quizzing older members of your family and getting as much information as you can by that means first. Documents in your family's possession may help fill out the picture. Few families, perhaps, are fortunate enough to have an ancient family Bible in which each generation's names have been carefully inscribed, but many will have other items of memorabilia, such as photograph albums, certificates or old letters and diaries from which to gain clues.

Family records

In terms of simply working out a family tree you can, of course, consult the records of Births, Deaths and Marriages (often known as BDMs), also held at the Family Records Centre, and probably travel back fairly easily to 1837 when registration began in England and Wales. Registration did not begin until 1855 in Scotland. Beyond that point you will be dependent on parish registers, some 10,000 transcripts of which are held by the Society of Genealogists. The IGI is made up of material largely taken from parish registers, though this is limited to baptisms and marriages, so is slightly less informative than parish registers, which will record burials and sometimes other events as well.

Schools and Apprenticeship records are more difficult to track down, as some are still in the possession of the institutions themselves, in local or county education offices or libraries. The Public Record Office, the Guildhall Library and the Society of Genealogists may all be able to help. Army, Navy, Police and Criminal records are also held at the Public Record Office, as are details of tax returns from the Domesday Book onwards.

It is in this sort of area that making use of the internet really comes into its own. As already explained, you can't yet read the contents of very many actual documents online but, most important, you can find out which documents are held where. Somewhere in this book you will certainly find a web site that will tell you where your local or county library is and which records it holds. Another will direct you to your nearest Family History Society. Others will tell you which national bodies hold records that you need to consult. Armed with that information you can plan a visit in person to consult such records, having already saved yourself an enormous amount of time by identifying in advance exactly what you want to see. Alternatively, in many cases you can make use of a service that will send you copies. Several such reputable services can be accessed online and not all of them are costly. Some will perform limited searches on your behalf free of charge.

Tutorials on the web

Another way in which you can make use of websites reviewed here is for learning more about the methodology of family research. GENUKI, for example, offers an excellent online introduction to the whole matter entitled 'Getting Started in Genealogy and Family History'. You may find it worthwhile to print off these seven pages and keep them by you as you get underway. They do deliver the warning that such notes are no substitute for 'good old-fashioned books' and, as you get more deeply into the quest, you will almost certainly find that you do need to consult books as well, but these notes are still a good way of setting the scene.

There are many other websites here that offer similar tutorial articles. It may be worth mentioning that, for the UK-based researcher, it is probably more relevant to make use of a British website for such purposes, rather than an American one. This is not to suggest for a moment that American-based tutorials are unreliable, since in general terms they will give you all the same very sound advice. However, they will not direct you to the right data sources unless you have established at some stage in your search that you are looking to consult British records (assuming this is the case). As a rough guide, URLs that end '.uk' will, of course be British. Those that end '.org' may well be British, and will be public bodies. Those that end '.com' are more likely to be American.

Having established that genealogy means going backwards in time, and family history means going outwards in exploration, where do you go next? It would be convenient if the websites on the internet fell neatly into those two categories. They don't. Many of them are not what you would call 'neatly contained' at all. With some 80,000 genealogical websites already posted and more being added every day, the opportunities for sites to assemble a multiplicity of links and become massively sprawling, all-things-to-all-men, gallimaufries of information are enormous.

Right at the beginning, the difficulty of classifying websites becomes evident. It seems obvious, for instance, that Family Search, the website that contains the IGI, should head the Searching for Names chapter. In fact, when you start consulting it you discover that it contains a great deal of other information, too, under a catch-all link entitled 'Browse Categories'. This, in turn, leads to a list of countries. From this massive databank you can review the records held in each country: a feature that earns this amazing website a place in the first, general section of this book.

Because of this difficulty of classification, do explore all the chapters here. In almost any of the websites reviewed you will find things that will either help or, at the very least, intrigue you. Some will enthral you, some will amuse. There really is a huge variety out there. I hope, having sifted out some of the less helpful ones, that not too many will infuriate you. Happy hunting!

Moving around the internet

How to move around large websites on the internet

People already familiar with using the internet, though not necessarily for genealogical research, will probably find that much of what follows is obvious. But those who have never explored the internet as a resource before may be glad of some help, particularly as so many genealogical web sites are extremely large. So I make no apology for the next few paragraphs. Those who know it all already can skip them.

First and foremost there is the absolute necessity of typing the URL (website address) correctly. Any error, however minor, will produce a 'page unavailable' notice. So the first thing to check, if there is a problem, is that the address has been entered correctly.

Once you have opened a website and started moving through it, the quickest way back to any earlier pages is to use the Back button at the top left of the page to retrace your steps. Alternatively, look for words such as 'home' or 'main' to return to the 'front' page (usually known as the homepage and always referred to as such here).

Scrolling down any given page can be done by two methods. One way is to click repeatedly on the up and down arrows in the right-hand toolbar, which allows you to move slowly and deliberately. To move much more rapidly, click and hold on the block between the two arrows and then slide it up or down the bar to the required new position and release. To move a whole page at a time, you can use the 'page up' and 'page down' buttons on your keyboard. Alternatively, clicking in the scroll bar just below the block will produce an automatic 'page down' result.

Sometimes, in the case of very long pages or lists, you may be scrolling through rapidly and appear to come to the end of your options before the list is complete. If the scroll block won't continue down the bar, you should probably just wait a few moments, during which the block will move back up the bar, to give the remainder of the page time to load.

Clicking on a 'link' means moving your cursor to either the relevant picture or words on the screen and clicking rapidly, usually twice with the principal (left-hand) button on your mouse. The link will then usually become highlighted, underlined and/or change colour. When an egg-timer symbol appears this means things are happening, whereas reverting to the cursor arrow or a hand means they are not.

Sometimes, clicking on a link will bring up a new, superimposed window. When this happens, you will probably need to enlarge the picture in order to read all the text. You do this by clicking in the 'maximise' square, which is the middle button of the three at the extreme right of the top-of-page toolbar. Once you have made use of the new information, you can either exit (right-hand button of the three) or minimise (left-hand button). Minimising rather than exiting will leave the name of the website just visited still visible in the bottom-of-page toolbar, which means you can re-open it quickly if you need to. Exiting, on the other hand, would mean that to return you would have to open it from scratch again.

Many of the websites in this book offer a 'Search' facility. If a search box has no 'go', 'search', 'find' or similar button, press the return key on your keyboard to initiate a search. Indeed, it is often quicker to do it this way, though you will find that a few search facilities insist on your using the button provided. Some searches require you to fill a succession of boxes with information before a search can be activated. Moving through a sequence of this sort can often be done more quickly by using the 'tab' key (above 'Caps Lock') on your keyboard than by moving the cursor each time with the mouse. Incidentally, many such sequences mark the compulsory boxes, as opposed to those you can leave blank, with an asterisk or similar device.

To leave one website and move to a completely new one, put the cursor in the 'Address' box at the top of the page and click with the left-hand mouse button once. This will highlight the current address and, as soon as you start typing, the address of the new site will immediately replace it.

It is not necessary to type 'http//' each time - simply type exactly the letters that appear as the URL in this book,

usually starting with 'www'. It is not normally necessary to observe capital letters. Simply pressing return on your keyboard, or 'go' if you prefer, will trigger the search for that website.

Once a website is open, its name will appear (probably in an abbreviated form) at the very bottom of your on-screen page, somewhere between 'Start' on the extreme left and the clock on the extreme right. If you open several sites, or windows, simultaneously, you can use these newly created name-buttons to move between them.

If a website comes up as unavailable, clicking on the word 'Refresh' very seldom sorts the problem, though it is always worth one try. Normally, it is better to abandon the quest and return on a later occasion, though do check before you leave that you have typed the site address correctly. Browsers vary in the cleverness with which they manage to find incorrectly addressed sites. If you find you have indeed made an error in the address, click on the address box twice rather than once, dismissing the highlighting, and then alter the necessary letters before pressing return or clicking on 'go' to try again.

Using a search engine to find the names of likely sites of interest is going to be one of the principal ways in which you use the internet for your genealogical researches. There are numerous portals (search engines restricted to specific fields of interest), general search engines, and meta-search engines (which search, in a single operation, the resources of many general search engines) available to you. I have my doubts about the usefulness of meta-searchers, because they normally 'present' your question to the individual search engines by means of a single, universal method, and this may not always work. They can then appear to have searched many different resources, without actually having done so. If you do decide to use a meta-searcher, one of the best is www.allsearchengines.com.

Good general search engines include Yahoo, Hotbot (now associated with Lycos), Altavista and so on. My preferred first choice is always www.Google.co.uk, for the following reasons: first, it is quick; second, it doesn't clutter its pages with advertisements; third, it lists the most likely matches first; fourth, and very importantly, it gives you a brief guide to what each website is about; and, finally, if you know the title of the organisation you are seeking but don't know the online address, you can try clicking on the 'I'm Feeling Lucky' button rather than the normal 'Search' button. Usually you will then hop to the relevant web site immediately. By the way, remember to use '.co.uk' after the search engine name wherever it applies – though if you try it with Hotbot (for which the correct address is '.com'), you will find that some canny entrepreneur has grabbed the name and is offering you furry hot water bottles!

On the whole, websites are surprisingly forgiving. If you start loading a page and, as soon as you see the first part of it, realise it is not what you want, you don't have to wait for it to finish loading completely before going elsewhere. You can use your back button or, if the index you came from is still visible, click on an alternative link before the 'wrong' page is complete. You may think this would cause a crash but in practice it very seldom does.

Many search facilities, both those of general search engines and those within individual web sites, will allow the use of some linking words, typically 'and', 'or' and 'not'. Some don't, though, and some (Google is one) assume 'and' automatically if there are two or more words in the search and inform you rather condescendingly that using it is unnecessary. In addition, some (such as Lycos advanced search) offer options such as 'the exact phrase' or 'all the words in any order'. This latter is useful when, for instance, you are looking for a name but don't know for certain how it will be presented, whether as 'John William Smith' or as 'Smith, John William'. Often, you can only find out how sophisticated any given search is by experimenting.

At various points you may be offered downloadable documents that are only readable if you have an Adobe Acrobat Reader. In these instances you are normally offered the relevant button for obtaining the reader on the spot. Clicking on it brings up a new window, with a long list of versions of the reader, from which you select 'Acrobat Reader - Windows' (unless you are working with an Apple Macintosh or another operating system). Now you are offered a new list from which you select the most appropriate version, typically in English (either with or without 'search' depending on how much memory you have available — with 'search' it takes about 6 megabytes) and the most recent date. The next stage is to fill in a name and email address, after which you can again instruct to download. Wait for another window to appear, in which you check that you are downloading to disk, and click again.

A lengthy transmission process will now ensue, taking probably half an hour or so, during which your window will show pages 'flying' from the globe on the left into an open yellow file. Having done all this, you then have to find the file in your hard drive, going in through Windows Explorer or equivalent. It will be pretty recognisable anyway because of the large memory requirement, and will be in there under a title something like 'rs405eng'. Double click on that to 'unzip' it, and follow instructions. Now, returning to the file you originally wanted to download and read, you should have no problem.

Finally, I refer you to a very useful, relatively recently posted web site called Newbies Helping Newbies. A group of friends in Forbes, New South Wales, Australia has been meeting for some time to pool their collective knowledge of computers and share their enjoyment of genealogy. The next obvious step was to put their assembled information together in a computer-accessible form, initially just for use by themselves and others who asked. Now the Newbies have a website, which is a model of clarity and does a remarkably good job of de-mystifying both the Internet as a whole and genealogy web sites in particular. For de-bugging problems of internet use, they are especially helpful. The genealogy stuff is, of course, written from an Australian starting point, though it is still very good. See Newbies Helping Newbies at www.angelfire.com/mt/forbesnewbies/index.html.

Saving time and money

A concern for many genealogy or family history researchers using the internet will be the amount of time spent online and the consequent cost. There are various ways of limiting this. For a start, of course, you may or may not be paying for your ISP. But even if you use a free provider, you are probably still being charged for the time spent online, in line with local call telephone charges. Using the internet after 6pm or at weekends is usually cheaper than during weekday daytimes. Unfortunately, of course, these tend to be the busiest times because everyone else in Britain (and more than a third of the homes in the country now have internet access) is doing the same, so you are likely to find that connections are slower and downloading individual web sites takes longer.

Once you have made a connection, remember that you have automatically spent the basic charge (currently around 4p) anyway, so you may as well make use of your time up to that value. At the best off-peak periods this may be as much as four minutes. The best way of mitigating the costs thereafter is probably to click on all the pages of a website that you think you are going to find useful, opening them sequentially but not actually spending time reading your way through them, and then close your connection. For a period, certainly for hours and perhaps up to a week, depending on the amount of memory dedicated to your cache (or 'Temporary Internet Files' if you're using Internet Explorer), you will find that you probably still have access to these areas and can trawl around at your leisure. You need

to select the 'Browse Offline' option. Even if you find that there are further pages you should have opened, it will be cheaper to go online again for a short period to do so, rather than stay online throughout your use of the site. To ensure that a page you may want to return to is not automatically deleted as your cache fills up, from the File menu use the 'Save As' option, which will allow you to save the page to your hard disk. Or you can always use the Print option from the File menu of your browser to print out a copy of a page.

If you quit, switch off and then want to return later, simply click on the down arrow to the right of your address box when you go back online and this will bring up a list of the most recently visited sites. An alternative to re-finding sites in this way is 'bookmarking' them (selecting 'Favorites' from above the address box and then clicking on 'Add to Favorites'), but this is probably best reserved for those sites that do indeed turn out to be your favourites over time.

If you find that the genealogy bug becomes life-dominating (and many have!), you may want to think about seeking not only a free ISP but also free online time. It's not totally free, of course, because you do pay a join-up fee or an annual subscription. For the purposes of writing this book, when I realised that I would be racking up a massive phone bill if I didn't do something radical, I decided to link to a service that would give me unlimited online time 24-hours-a-day for a year. I found the one I am using by putting the words 'free Internet UK' into a search engine (the UK bit is important).

Some such services send you an adapter through the post that you apply to your telephone but others allow you to sign up online immediately, paying by credit card. I chose one of the latter and the service is proving highly satisfactory. Meanwhile, although I had to pay to subscribe, I didn't hesitate once I worked out that I would otherwise have spent the same amount of money using the internet within my first three days!

If you decide not to follow this route, and are consequently still paying for your online time, you may like to consult the chapter entitled 'How to Move Around Large Websites on the Internet', in the hope of picking up some tips on such things as rapid scrolling through sites, quick filling of search boxes and so on. In any case, one of the things that will be most useful in the long term is simple familiarity with the way the internet works. After that point, the next stage is familiarity with how typical genealogical web sites work, because very many of them are extremely similar in the way they operate. Good luck!

Chapter 2

general genealogy sites

In this chapter you will find the websites of major organisations that are likely to be central to your research, as well as some smaller ones that either offer good tutorial assistance or list a large number of relevant links. Some of these websites are so extensive that it is only possible to give a glimpse of their riches. You will simply have to spend some time exploring them to discover the full range of information they provide.

The difficulty of categorisation has already been mentioned. Many of the websites listed in this chapter could also have entries elsewhere, for instance, when they present online links to book or software sales, to research assistance, to libraries, or when they publish a magazine. Meanwhile, RootsWeb, which opens the Searching For Names chapter (see p. 71), and other similar websites could also have appeared here. The chapter categories are a guide, therefore, and not a rigid system dividing one type of website from another.

It is also important to understand the system of ordering used for the reviews. The Good Web Guide's policy, which is followed here, is to list websites with a five-star overall rating first, then the four-star sites, and so on. Where several sites earn the same rating, they are then listed alphabetically. The star ratings relate not only to the content of each website, but also to the ease, or otherwise, of using it. Points for readability, navigation and speed are clearly issues of practical use, whereas I have taken updating, content and overall rating to be more related to a qualitative assessment of the material for the purposes of UK-based genealogical research. This means that websites that may be excellent in themselves but are of only limited use to the genealogist will rate an overall lower star score accordingly. Please don't avoid them, however, or you may miss out on a nugget of pure gold.

www.bbc.co.uk/history/programmes/blood			
Bloodties			
Overall rating: ★ ★ ★ ★ ★			
Classification:	General	Readability:	★ ★ ★ ★ ★
Updating:	Occasionally	Content:	★ ★ ★ ★
Navigation:	★ ★ ★ ★ ★	Speed:	★ ★ ★ ★ ★
UK			

This is the website associated with BBC2's Bloodties programme. It is fortunate that both by star-rating and by alphabetical order it comes first, as it offers one of the best introductions to the whole business of doing UK-based family history research on the entire web. Warning: clicking on any of the headings under 'Find' at the top of the purple, left-of-page margin will take you to the main BBC website, which is not what you want. Move only between the links under 'Jump To'.

SPECIAL FEATURES

Bloodties Click on this first. It appears in the list under 'Jump To' in the left-of-page purple margin. The explanations here of how to set about family history research for the first time ever are clear, sensible and unpatronising.

Heraldry/Coats of Arms are two similarly clear explanatory pages.

History is interesting but probably only of use if it happens to address a topic you are researching, because it is centred on the BBC's own recent programmes rather than being a directory of history resources in general.

Links leads to good basic lists of all the major websites (detailed elsewhere in this book), helpfully divided by country: England and Wales first, then Scotland, then

Northern Ireland and the Republic of Ireland. At the bottom of the same page is an especially good list of websites to consult in connection with Victorian photographs. This area is further explored in Snap Shots, Crime Photos and Mug Shots, also in the purple index. The last of these contains some rather poignant images.

BBC Knowledge is effectively the BBC's online schools encyclopaedia.

What a wonderful starting point. It deserves exploration by any new-to-genealogy researcher.

www.cyndislist.com
Cyndi's List of Genealogy Sites on the Internet

Overall rating: ★ ★ ★ ★			
Classification:	General	**Readability:**	★ ★ ★ ★ ★
Updating:	Regularly	**Content:**	★ ★ ★ ★
Navigation:	★ ★ ★ ★	**Speed:**	★ ★ ★ ★ ★

US

This vast, extraordinary website is run by the amazing Cyndi Howells, genealogy obsessive and family-loving, all-American mom. Predominantly purple in colour, with shadowy red oak leaves scattered around each page, it's friendly, chatty and personal in what most UK users will think a very American style. BUT, listing as it does every genealogy website she knows, it's an absolute mine of information. At the time of writing Cyndi is receiving something like 200 emails every day, half of which she answers immediately. She has posted nearly 80,000 sites and has just welcomed her ten millionth visitor.

Cheerful-looking husband Mark has put together what UK users may well find is one of the most useful parts of the site. 'Researching Ancestors from the United Kingdom' (his picture's available under 'About Mark Howells' at the end of the article) is a seven-page run-down of how to get going, which you may find worthwhile to print off. To find this, go to FAQs, then Personal Questions (bottom of page), then Mark and Cyndi's Family Tree, then Mark's Research, Including the UK & Ireland, and, finally, to the required article. The complexity of the route tells you something about the complexity of the site as a whole.

Overall, the site would have merited five stars in every category, except that Cyndi herself gives several very sensible warnings about trusting the information supplied, as it is simply not possible for her to check the reliability of everything submitted. On top of all this, she and Mark have a baby son called Evan, the newest 'twig' on the family tree, who gets lots of pictures, too. How on earth do they manage it? Oh, and it's all free.

SPECIAL FEATURES

Cyndi's List – THE BOOK! and **Netting Your Ancestors** are links to online order forms for Cyndi's two books, detailed here with all the reviews that have attended their publication. A third book-ordering link is to Amazon.com Genealogy Bookstore. A fourth takes you to Heritage Quest Magazine, an American periodical perhaps not of great relevance to UK users but available at a reduced subscription to users of Cyndi's List.

Cyndi's List Category Indexes & Search Engine offers her entire list of websites sorted in a number of different ways, such as in a 'No-Frills' form, by alphabetical order or by topics, a useful first method of sifting through this vast resource.

What's New on Cyndi's List? details all the new sites submitted in recent days. Within the first two days of the month visited, nearly 50 new sites had been posted!

CyndisList Mailing List gives details of how to become a subscriber, while How to Submit a New Link to Cyndi's List is self-explanatory.

Internet Stuff You Need to Know gives some very worthwhile warnings about such annoyances as spam, chain-letters, hoaxes and computer viruses, as well as helpful tips on terminology, netiquette, search engines and privacy issues.

Cyndi's Genealogy Home Page Construction Kit is just what it says: a guide to creating your own family tree homepage, with lists of free or reasonably priced page-hosting services, to putting your details into a GEDCOM format, designing a

website either yourself or using a professional, and such important things as how to cope with updating and where to advertise your website.

The links available from this site are almost too numerous to comprehend, so the best starting point is probably Frequently Asked Questions. Under 'Why do you do all this?', Cyndi answers, 'because I have fun', and also neatly explains what Cyndi's List is: '... the internet is like a library with its books strewn all over the floor. I guess I'd like my list to be the card catalog for the genealogy section of that library.'

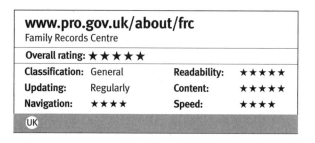

www.pro.gov.uk/about/frc
Family Records Centre

Overall rating: ★ ★ ★ ★			
Classification: General		**Readability:**	★ ★ ★ ★ ★
Updating: Regularly		**Content:**	★ ★ ★ ★ ★
Navigation: ★ ★ ★ ★		**Speed:**	★ ★ ★ ★

UK

On 16 May 2000, the critically important and relatively recently established FRC finally got a banner headline on the homepage of the Public Record Office, one of whose jewels in the crown it surely is (it can also be found, admittedly, under the Genealogy link). It has, in fact, won the first-ever Prince Michael of Kent Award for excellence in family history, awarded by the Society of Genealogists.

The Family Records Centre was established in 1997 by the PRO and the Office for National Statistics. The core of its collections is made up of records of births, marriages, deaths and adoptions, previously held at the General Register Office in St Catherine's House, London, and census returns for England and Wales, previously held at the PRO itself in Chancery Lane. FRC Services is the link that will give you some immediate background information about these collections, and is now available to be consulted at the FRC's premises in Myddelton Street, London.

SPECIAL FEATURES

FRC Newsletters are available to be read online.

FRC Leaflets leads to a list of half a dozen leaflets on such topics as Censuses, Wills and Probate and Tracing Missing Persons. Each of these is also available to be read online and offers further internal links, so they are well worth investigating.

1901 Census Project will give regular updates on the recently awarded project (to DERA) to digitise what will soon be the most recently released census – an exciting development.

Genealogy, at the bottom of the homepage, offers further helpful links, including Resources for Genealogists, which is a very useful list.

Incidentally, the PRO produces an extremely good and attractively illustrated booklet called 'The Family Records Centre Introduction to Family History'. Costing £3.99, it is available from the PRO itself (see p. 35).

THE vital resource, sooner or later, for all genealogists. A good deal of the same online information can be accessed through the Public Record Office website (see p. 35), but this is a more direct route.

Here you will find the famous IGI (International Genealogical Index), popularly but incorrectly called the Mormon Index, created by the members of the Church of Jesus Christ of Latter-Day Saints, whose headquarters is in Salt Lake City, Utah. On your first visit it might be worth consulting About the Church of Jesus Christ of Latter-Day Saints (left-hand column) just to understand what this is all about, but be warned that loading is somewhat slow. In no doubt simplified terms, members of the Church believe that they can baptise ancestors, posthumously, into the Mormon faith, so to find those ancestors they are building up a massive database of family history records. Some record holders, for instance, a few Church of England parish priests, have refused access, so those records have not been transcribed. The great majority, however, have been amenable and the result is the most massive, free, online genealogical database in the world.

SPECIAL FEATURES

Search For Ancestors in the left-hand column offers you an immediate opportunity to start searching. Provided you know the name(s) you are looking for, you don't need to worry about filling in further details of dates and events unless you are very certain of them, otherwise you may get less information rather than more. The only 'required' boxes are the first and last names (indicated by the asterisks above them), though adding the country certainly helps. Having

filled in the necessary, go immediately to 'search' and refine your quest from the list that you are then offered. Tips for searching are offered from a link in purple letters just above the search boxes.

Browse Categories introduces you to some of the other phenomenal riches of this website, under further links such as **Census and Lists, Court and Legal Records, Cultural and Religious Groups, Military, Land** and **Property,** and several others. Here you select any of the above categories and you are then immediately offered a list of world countries, from which you select those whose records you wish to review. Incidentally, British records are listed under Great Britain, not United Kingdom. It is true to say that the lists that then appear need to be approached with a good deal of selectivity. Small, local family history societies are mixed up with major record-holding bodies, in no logical order, and there are some out-of-date inaccuracies. For instance, it is claimed that vital records are held at the General Records Office in St Catherine's House, London, whereas it was, of course, called the General Register Office, and, in any case, those records are now at the Family Records Centre in Myddelton Street. As a route to the records of other countries, however, this still has to be considered a very valuable starting point.

Collaborate with Others, Preserve Your Genealogy, Add a Site and Feedback all require registration to participate but, once you have your own records in order, you may well feel it worthwhile to do so.

Order Family History Resources does what it says, offering you the opportunity to order publications, software and other supplies. If you think you can't get back to the homepage from here, click on the FamilySearch logo above the pictorial box.

Help is where to find Frequently Asked Questions and various other links, most already available from the homepage index. It also contains the very useful Getting Started pages, which give step-by-step instructions if you are still in any difficulty. You will probably need to use the 'maximise' button on your top toolbar to read these instructions comfortably.

This is the real thing, the most indispensable online resource on the entire web. And it grows more and more impressive daily (look at What's New at the top of the left-hand margin).

www.ffhs.org.uk
Federation of Family History Societies

Overall rating: ★ ★ ★ ★ ★

Classification:	General	Readability:	★ ★ ★ ★ ★
Updating:	Regularly	Content:	★ ★ ★ ★
Navigation:	★ ★ ★ ★ ★	Speed:	★ ★ ★ ★

UK

Formed in 1974, the Federation now has a membership of around 200 societies, some national, some regional, and some that represent only one-name studies. Their twice-yearly journal is Family History News and Digest, but they also publish a number of books and information leaflets. All member societies receive a copy of the Handbook, in which each of them automatically receives a listing. Among projects currently being supported are the National Inventory of War Memorials and continuing work on the indexing of census returns and other records. The Federation also runs courses and conferences, and represents the interests of its membership at national level.

SPECIAL FEATURES

First Steps Situated on the homepage, click on 'If you're starting out on British Genealogy', which is where you will find Your Questions, always a good route to discovering what any particular organisation does.

Research Services explains that many societies do not have the resources to cope with the vast number of queries that are put to them, and outlines the ways in which you, as a person requesting information, can help by making your enquiry as clear as possible. Given that their work is normally done free of charge, it is particularly important that you observe these recommendations and are not too impatient about getting immediate answers.

The Strays Clearing House and the National Strays Index form a vital resource for those seeking ancestors who are difficult to track because, for whatever reason, they are recorded as being 'from' or connected with somewhere other than the area in which they normally lived. As the excellent explanatory notes say, these records are 'greatly under-used'. Sometimes they contain the vital clue that de-bugs a long-standing problem. They can't be consulted online, but your nearest FHS will have them on microfiche, or you can order them from the Federation – instructions are provided at the bottom of the page.

Tracing the Birth Parents of Adopted Persons is self-explanatory, and the Federation may be able to help when other searches have failed, as the page explains.

You and Your Record Office offers excellent advice on how to prepare for a visit to your County Record Office and make the most of your time there.

In Search of your Soldier Ancestors is a very clear guide to the whereabouts and contents of military records.

And Finally..., at the bottom of the homepage, mentions two other important matters. You can apply, online, for the newly launched 'Ancestry' patio rose and, even if you are not a rose grower, you can contribute to BIG-R, the British Isles Genealogical Register, a special project for the millennium. Do investigate.

A vital website for any family history enthusiast, which should persuade you of the value of joining your local FHS.

www.genuki.org.uk

GENUKI: The UK & Ireland Genealogical Information Service

Overall rating: ★ ★ ★ ★ ★			
Classification:	General	Readability:	★ ★ ★ ★ ★
Updating:	Regularly	Content:	★ ★ ★ ★
Navigation:	★ ★ ★ ★ ★	Speed:	★ ★ ★ ★ ★

UK

Without question the most important website of general use to UK researchers, GENUKI is a 'virtual reference library' of genealogical data. It is important to understand that this is a library of primary source material, drawn from historical documentation, and is not secondary (or tertiary – see Introduction) material such as GEDCOM files assembled by individuals. To get an immediate idea of its massive scope, click on the logo in the central box.

SPECIAL FEATURES

Guidance for First-Time Users is the best place to start. Under the heading 'How this information server is organised', the second paragraph contains a link to 'standards observed by each of the providers', and it is these that earn GENUKI its high reliability rating. Further down the page is Published Papers about this Server which, if you still need convincing, should demonstrate why this website is held in such high regard worldwide.

Getting Started in Genealogy, in the yellow boxes in the middle of the page, comprises an article and bibliography to inform those researching family history for the first time.

FAQs is exceptionally useful, and possibly a more immediately informative place to start exploring the site than through Contents at top right of the homepage, which leads mainly to a list of British and Irish counties.

Contents, however, has vital information slightly 'buried' in the first few lines. First, at the bottom of the introductory paragraph, there is a link to the GENUKI Search Engine, which will search all GENUKI pages. And immediately below that is an apparent repeat of GENUKI Contents, which does admittedly say 'not to be overlooked'. True indeed, as you will see when you look at it.

GENEVA is the list of forthcoming or, as they put it with a gentle nod to American users, 'upcoming' events which appears in the last of the yellow boxes. If the issue of language differences amuses you, try clicking on the top right yellow box, Researching UK and Irish Genealogy from Abroad, and then click on Brit-Speak (English as a second language for Americans) at the end of the Introduction.

The most complete, most user-friendly general site for British users. If you can't find anything to help you here, you're in trouble indeed.

www.pro.gov.uk
The Public Record Office

Overall rating: ★ ★ ★ ★			
Classification: General		**Readability:**	★ ★ ★ ★ ★
Updating:	Regularly	**Content:**	★ ★ ★ ★
Navigation:	★ ★ ★	**Speed:**	★ ★ ★ ★

UK

The PRO itself says 'it will inspire and inform you at all stages of your family history detective work'. Its homepage lists a number of recent announcements under red date-strips in the middle of the page. On a recent look, these included information about the Access to Archives project, the PRO's new Education and Visitor Centre, and details of forthcoming exhibitions and recently received awards.

SPECIAL FEATURES

In the small picture blocks to either side of the page are the links to the PRO's regular information. These operate quickly to take you to further explanations of what the PRO's functions are and what records it holds. The somewhat elliptical titles to the boxes are not all that informative, and the boxes sometimes don't contain what you'd expect.

Finding Aids, top right picture box, leads to a link heading the next page, New Catalogue Users Start Here. This will, in fact, probably be the best place to start. Other useful boxes to explore are Genealogy, on the left, and Bookshop and Events, on the right. Finding one's way around even from these starting points is still quite complicated and takes a certain amount of persistence, but the records held are sufficiently important to reward the effort.

Readers Click here, in the left-of-page picture boxes, once you have decided that a visit is required. This tells you about public access, which is important because all research is done in person. No original documents or facsimiles are available yet for consultation online.

Among the principal sources of records for any genealogist, the PRO website is attractive and well worth exploring in some detail.

www.sog.org.uk
The Society of Genealogists

Overall rating: ★ ★ ★ ★

Classification:	General	Readability:	★★★★★
Updating:	Regularly	Content:	★★★★★
Navigation:	★★★★	Speed:	★★★★★

(UK)

The Society of Genealogists is a charity whose object is to support, both by research facilities and personal guidance, those interested in tracing their family history. The homepage offers links to the Society's Library (see below), Events, the Society's Bookshop (in Charterhouse Buildings, near the Barbican in London) and its On-line Bookshop, which operates in a conventional manner. The About the Society page has indicated for nearly a year that membership will be available online in due course; in fact, it is there already if you click on Membership, either at the bottom of this page or as the second entry on the homepage. An email address is also given. All links are exceptionally clear and, without images, speed is excellent. Updating seems to be almost entirely in the hands of Peter Christian, who must be working night and day to keep abreast of things.

SPECIAL FEATURES

Library is a massive resource, with over 9,000 Parish Registers, County Records, Census material, Poll Books and Directories. It also contains much material on the professions, the services, the peerage, religious denominations, schools and universities – an absolutely essential starting point. Particularly useful is the 'Before Coming to the Library' advice, which suggests preparatory work you should do to make your visit more productive. Similarly, clicking on 'Arrangement of the Building' will give you advance notice of how to find your way around. This link is actually a good way of discovering in general terms what the Library contains. Money from the Heritage Lottery Fund is used to computerise the catalogue, and a progress report on this is found under Projects.

Events gives information about the Society's lectures and courses, most of which are held at their own premises in London, with some further afield, as well as visits to such places as The College of Arms, the Theatre Museum and Library, London's 'Little Venice', the Inns of Court and the Royal College of Surgeons Library. It also gives details of major Family History Fairs, both in London and elsewhere.

Projects includes the plan to publish surname indexes to the marriage licences issued by both the Vicar General (1694–1850) and the Master of Faculties (1714–1850) of the Archbishop of Canterbury. The first of these is already available in book and microfiche form, and electronic publishing is a likely next stage. This massive work is being done by volunteers.

The Society On-line gives details of mailing lists, hosted by RootsWeb, and other online material currently available.

Genealogists' Magazine and **Computers in Genealogy** are links to the Society's own publications, with good details of the contents of both current and past issues. Articles and reviews that are over a year old can be read online.

Links, at the very bottom of the list on the homepage, is actually a way in to a very useful page headed 'Essential websites'. Bookmarking this as a first-stop entry point might be a very natty, shortcut way of accessing many other highly useful organisations, without the need to list them all individually. Have a look and see what you think.

A brilliantly simple, rapid site for finding out what material the Society owns, where to find it and what other organisations to approach.

www.accessgenealogy.com
Access Genealogy

Overall rating: ★ ★ ★ ★			
Classification:	General	**Readability:**	★★★★
Updating:	Regularly	**Content:**	★★★
Navigation:	★★★★	**Speed:**	★★★★

US

The object here is to shortcut the routes to a mass of records (currently 2 billion, they say) that are held both in the US and the UK.

SPECIAL FEATURES

Ancestry Clicking here on the left-hand side of the homepage takes you to Ancestry.com, while the other links are to the associated websites, MyFamily.com and FamilyHistory.com. In the right-hand half of the page, however, are the links to UK records, listed initially by county. Clicking on several counties to test the system produced useful information about where to find local records, provided as a result of linking to GENUKI (see p. 34).

The style of this website is correctly defined by its title 'Access Genealogy'. Probably everything available here for the UK is equally readily available from GENUKI, but here you can move quickly between UK and US records, starting from the same homepage, which could prove useful.

www.excite.co.uk/lifestyle
Excite Lifestyle

Overall rating: ★ ★ ★ ★			
Classification:	General	**Readability:**	★ ★ ★ ★
Updating:	Occasionally	**Content:**	★ ★ ★ ★
Navigation:	★ ★ ★ ★	**Speed:**	★ ★ ★ ★

UK

This is a major search engine that has an area specifically devoted to genealogy.

SPECIAL FEATURES

Genealogy Clicking on this, the first of the links under Lifestyle in the left-hand column, brings up a useful list of websites, mostly on specific topics from within GENUKI. Some are independent of GENUKI, addressing such areas as Census Finding Aids (linking to Ron Taylor's useful rontay.digiweb.com website) and Quaker Genealogical Resources (going to quaker.org.uk/geneal.html).

Organisations and Societies/Getting Professional Help Additional links can be found under these headings further down the page.

At the bottom left of the page is a search box where you can name any family tree software (but not FamilyTreeMaker, which is listed further up the page under 'Excite Favourites') for a star-rated assessment. If you want to compare them all, simply leave the search box blank and click on 'Search'. You can then look at any particular one in more detail.

A useful search-engine facility with real genealogical value and some unexpected links.

www.familytreemaker.com
Family Tree Maker

Overall rating: ★ ★ ★ ★			
Classification:	General	**Readability:**	★ ★ ★ ★
Updating:	Regularly	**Content:**	★ ★
Navigation:	★ ★ ★ ★	**Speed:**	★ ★ ★

US R

Widely known as one of the best software applications for storing family history records, FamilyTreeMaker also offers this gateway website with a load of useful information and numerous links to other supportive organisations. The international nature of the enterprise makes this possibly not the best starting point for UK users, but it is still a site that is worth exploring. (For information about the FamilyTreeMaker software application see p. 123.) The site is also available as www.bannerblue.com.

SPECIAL FEATURES

Find Family is the shortcut route to discovering whether there is any information here that may be of specific interest to you. Putting in the names of any ancestors you are seeking will produce rapid results, and, if you strike lucky, you can then click on the name of the in-putter, which will bring up an email facility whereby you can contact him or her. The fact that all information is input by enthusiasts inevitably risks compromising reliability, hence the modest star-rating above.

Family Archives, also linked from the homepage, is certainly worth some exploration.

Other links on the homepage are **World Family Tree** (on the whole, don't bother), **Community Center** (message boards, events listings), **Genealogy Help** (Step-by-Step Guide, classes, useful addresses) and opportunities to buy both FTM itself, or its upgrades, and books on genealogy.

Probably most useful will be either the **How-To Articles**, recently published magazine articles of which the current examples are listed further down the page, or the **Research Services**.

Record Lookup Services is what clicking on the latter produces, and where the professional staff of Genealogy Research Associates will look up records at your request (for a fee) and either photocopy or scan them for you. They will also offer advice. The list of records available includes US and Foreign Censuses, reports from the New York Times, Immigrant Ship Passenger Lists (including Irish to America between 1846 and 1851), details of Canadian Border Crossings, US Passport Applications 1860–1924, American Army records, American births, marriages, deaths and wills. Although the site is aimed at a mainly US audience, the staff are also prepared to look up British and other foreign records of the same type, although UK users would clearly find it more cost- and time-effective to seek these from a UK source, such as the Family Records Centre (see p. 31) in London.

Helpful Websites leads to Genealogy.com, the website maintained by April and Matt Helm (see next review), probably best known for their book, Genealogy Online for Dummies.

Unbeatable, in the view of many, as a software package, Family Tree Maker puts on a pretty good show at its internet address as well. The support available if you are tracking ancestors in the US is really valuable, especially as it is done by professionals. But you do have to pay, and getting results will take time.

www.genealogy.com

Genealogy.com and Genealogy Toolbox

Overall rating: ★ ★ ★ ★			
Classification: General		**Readability:**	★ ★ ★
Updating: Regularly		**Content:**	★ ★ ★
Navigation: ★ ★ ★ ★		**Speed:**	★ ★ ★ ★

US

Typical of American websites, the homepage for this one looks busy and even cluttered on first acquaintance. It is well organised, however, particularly as the card-file tabs along the top of the page reappear on every page you subsequently open, so moving between pages is easy and rapid. The site is maintained by April and Matthew Helm, co-authors of the book Genealogy Online for Dummies, one in a very popular and successful series that will probably be familiar to most readers.

SPECIAL FEATURES

New? Start Here immediately offers, in the middle of the page, a search box into which you can type the name of the ancestor you are researching, with the surname or 'last' name being the only one that is essential. Frustratingly, at the top of the resulting list there is no indication of the number of 'hits' the name has produced, so you are left to trawl through you know not how many pages, unless you can refine the search sufficiently to produce so few that they will fit on a single page.

Search for Family brings up a page headed Begin Your Family Research Online, which offers eight links, among them Social Security Death Index (USA), E-mail and Telephone Directories (also USA), where you can search for contact details for living relatives, and KnowX.com, another people-finding (alive or dead) facility.

Learn About Genealogy has some good ideas, starting with a link to Family Explorer, which is a useful and clear 'How to...' guide to building up, recording and sharing a personal family history. About two-thirds of the way down the list is an invaluable tool called Look it up in the Glossary, which takes you straight to a massive dictionary of archaic or legal terms, as well as commonly used abbreviations. Simply click on the letter that begins the term you are having problems with and then scroll down the alphabetical list to find it.

International, Ethnic and Religious Resources This is situated at the bottom of the Learn About Genealogy page. Clicking on the 'globe' button and then scrolling down to 'British' or 'Scotch-Irish', for instance, on the next page, produces some very useful contact addresses as well as suggested reading material.

Community Center offers, among other things, The Virtual Cemetery, where you can contribute an electronic memorial, adding photographs if you wish, or view an existing tombstone – an idea that may become very popular.

Helpful Websites offers a massive and extremely valuable Genealogy SiteFinder service, with headings sensibly laid out inside a blue-edged box, at the top of which is a photograph of the Helms. Usefully, the numbers in brackets after the headings indicate the number of websites available on each topic. Typing 'translation services' in the search box, for instance, immediately produced seven matches, listed in order of relevance and with detailed onward links.

Shopping, finally, takes you to the Genealogy Store. Clicking on Software, for example, takes you to a 'Which'-style comparative table for four of the most popular applications: Family Tree Maker, Family Tree Detective, Family Origins and Ultimate Family Tree. Shopping for Books brings up each title quickly with full details, including the publisher's 'blurb' but not, it seems, any objective reviews.

This is a big, big site with plenty of useful material to offer, which makes it a good place to start if you are going to tackle American sites at all. The online Glossary is particularly handy.

<table>
<tr><td colspan="2">www.zen.co.uk/home/page/news.htm
Joe's Genealogy 2000</td></tr>
<tr><td colspan="2">Overall rating: ★ ★ ★ ★</td></tr>
<tr><td>Classification: General</td><td>Readability: ★ ★ ★ ★</td></tr>
<tr><td>Updating: Occasionally</td><td>Content: ★ ★ ★</td></tr>
<tr><td>Navigation: ★ ★ ★ ★</td><td>Speed: ★ ★ ★ ★</td></tr>
<tr><td colspan="2">UK</td></tr>
</table>

Below the grey box that runs right across the homepage is a list of all the things Joe's website purveys, from his Hints for Beginners to See Where Joe is Doing a Talk, and a list of Joe's Guides or Other Shareware Genealogy Software.

SPECIAL FEATURES

Click on the blue 'Go' buttons to open any of the pages.

What's New! At the time of testing, this section offered the opportunity to check out the World's Top 100 Genealogy Sites, which was interesting to do, even though they proved to be predominantly American.

Surf Through Many Genealogy Related Web Sites Listed links to a lengthy and most useful list, though several of those tested proved unavailable. This, of course, is one of the hazards of doing research on the internet. When websites close down or are discontinued for whatever reason, usually nobody remembers to inform the search engines and portals where they have been listed.

The penultimate button allows you to sign up to receive Joe's free newsletters by email.

This is certainly worth exploring in some detail, partly for the helpful basic information logged here, and partly for the vast range of onward links.

<table>
<tr><td colspan="2">www.open.gov.uk
CCTA Government Information Service</td></tr>
<tr><td colspan="2">Overall rating: ★ ★ ★</td></tr>
<tr><td>Classification: General</td><td>Readability: ★ ★ ★</td></tr>
<tr><td>Updating: Regularly</td><td>Content: ★ ★ ★ ★</td></tr>
<tr><td>Navigation: ★ ★</td><td>Speed: ★ ★</td></tr>
<tr><td colspan="2">UK</td></tr>
</table>

Ironically, for the public gateway to the so-called Open Government website, this is positively one of the most unwelcoming homepages on the entire internet, with only two immediately evident links, both of which say 'do not follow this link unless...' the moment you approach them. In desperation, you click instead on the very small tabs along the top of the page, headed 'text navigation', and then you start to get somewhere. At the time of testing, clicking on 'search' brought up an as yet incomplete service, but it should become useful in due course.

SPECIAL FEATURES

Organisation Index, in the top-of-page tabs, is certainly the best place to start if you know the name of the organisation you are seeking. The first page of entries under the letter 'A' comes up automatically. To move to subsequent pages, click on the first letter of your sought organisation's name from the blue-lettered alphabet at the top of the page. One intelligent feature here is that the indexing allows for some vagueness. For instance, if you were looking for Scottish records and should be hunting for the General Register Office for Scotland but had not remembered that title correctly, clicking on 'S' rather than 'G' would still offer the right link.

Topic Index, also in the tiny tabs, produces a list of what might be termed generic categories, such as Agriculture,

Charities, Education, Foreign Affairs and so on. Among these is Public Records, which links to the Commonwealth War Graves Commission, Public Record Office and Companies House Records, though all of these can also be reached through the Organisation Index, too. Similarly, clicking on Scotland would be yet another route to finding the General Register Office for Scotland, so from the navigation point of view you would be unlucky if you did not eventually find what you were looking for.

The two indexes are extremely valuable, leading as they do to such a vast number of other organisations and their websites. The search facility is not yet one to put at the top of your list, but it should one day develop into something very useful.

http://gk.bored.org
GK Genealogy

Overall rating: ★ ★ ★

Classification:	General	**Readability:**	★ ★ ★
Updating:	Occasionally	**Content:**	★ ★ ★
Navigation:	★ ★ ★	**Speed:**	★ ★ ★

UK

This rather alarming-looking website on a black background offers a limited amount of information for the genealogist. To access what there is, use the left-hand margin index.

SPECIAL FEATURES

Scanned Birth Certificate, Death Certificate, Marriage Certificate, Census Return and **IGI Entries** One of the more interesting features here is the on-screen pictures of actual sample documents. Looking under any of these, if you have never seen one before, might be helpful, though the sample IGI entry is so small as to be pretty unreadable. Below this is a Java facility for calculating the day of the week on which any event in the past actually occurred. Then a list of Counties follows, with details of population related to overall area and population density.

Not a principal port of call but still one worth investigating, especially if you want to know the type of information you would get from consulting what are usually termed 'vital' records.

www.sarfas.co.uk
RS Designs

Overall rating: ★ ★ ★			
Classification: General		**Readability:**	★ ★ ★
Updating: Rarely		**Content:**	★ ★ ★
Navigation: ★ ★ ★		**Speed:**	★ ★

UK

Ray Sarfas has his own website here, with a homepage that is less than quick to load due to the ingenious pictures. Don't click on Genealogy unless you want to get involved in exploring the Sarfas family name. Instead, click on Information.

SPECIAL FEATURES

Information provides a useful list of links for genealogists, including a good index of local family history societies – though frustratingly not nearly as many as in Mr Sarfas' own booklet 'Genealogy Resources on the Internet'. The booklet, for those who are interested, may be ordered from RS Designs, 60 Grasmere, Macclesfield, Cheshire, SK11 8PL. It contains, like the online list here, only a list of website addresses – but it is a good list.

On the date tested, the website had not apparently been updated for nearly six months, but it nevertheless contained a useful list of other addresses, so is still worth investigation.

www.ukgenealogyusa.free-online.co.uk
UK Genealogy USA

Overall rating: ★ ★ ★			
Classification: General		**Readability:**	★ ★ ★ ★
Updating: Occasionally		**Content:**	★ ★ ★
Navigation: ★ ★ ★		**Speed:**	★ ★ ★

US

Aimed at the novice genealogist, the introductory pages here are, despite several misspellings, especially clear and simple, often using the 'An example would be...' technique of explaining further. As the homepage suggests, click on Genealogy (in purple letters) first, then on Where to Start at the bottom of that page.

SPECIAL FEATURES

Links in the tabs along the top of any page leads to links under three headings: Genealogy Sites, Software Sites and Other Sites. The lists that follow are not long but each is intelligently selective.

Services and Prices tell you about employing the partnership, run by Julie Henderson in the UK and Jo Koegel in the US (more details under About Us), to do research on your behalf. Rates are reasonable.

A useful place for the complete beginner to start.

www.origins.net
Origins.net

Overall rating: ★ ★			
Classification: General		**Readability:**	★ ★ ★
Updating: Regularly		**Content:**	★ ★ ★ ★
Navigation: ★ ★ ★		**Speed:**	★ ★ ★ ★

UK £ 🔒

Origins.net will clearly become an absolutely central resource for all genealogists in due course. Whether it will ever be quite as user-friendly as visiting the library of the Society of Genealogists in person is questionable, but the pressures on that organisation are becoming so intense that online research does seem to be the eventual, inevitable and only solution.

Founded in 1997, Origins.net has just secured a major new project under which the records of the Society of Genealogists (see p. 36) will be transferred to join the Scottish records that Origins already holds. Details of this development can be found at the moment by clicking on the Major New Announcement (red lettering) on the homepage. The fact that, as yet, only the Scottish records are available explains the overall two-star rating.

SPECIAL FEATURES

Visit Scots Origins now Clicking here brings up an index in three columns of grey boxes. The payment system will be the same as that currently in operation for the Scottish records. Much the most illuminating of these are demo and FAQ. To explain briefly, the system is that a user code is issued, you give your credit card details to the secure site, and are then issued with 30 page-credits to use in a 24-hour period. At present this costs £6. You now initiate a search and are told how many matches this has produced. If there are too many, you can try refining your search before actually downloading any individual pages to view. Each page you view uses one page-credit, and by paying again you can obtain 30 more page-credits at any time. You can save the results of a search by clicking on 'File' in your top toolbar and then selecting either 'Save As' or 'Print'.

Useful addresses

Family Records Centre
1 Myddelton Street
London
EC1R 1UW
tel: *Census and General Enquiries: 020 8392 5300*
        Births, Marriages, Deaths: 0151 471 4800
fax: *020 8392 5307*

Federation of Family History Societies
The Benson Room
Birmingham and Midland Institute
Margaret Street
Birmingham
B3 3BS
tel: *01704 149 032*

The Public Record Office
Kew
Richmond
Surrey
TW9 4DU
tel: *020 8392 5200*
fax: *020 8392 5286*

The Society of Genealogists
14 Charterhouse Buildings
Goswell Road
London
EC1M 7BA
tel: *020 7251 8799*
fax: *020 7250 1800*

UK Genealogy USA
52 Greenfoot Lane
Old Town
Barnsley
South Yorkshire
S75 2TA
tel: *01226 770304*
email: *call@ukgenealogyusa.idps.co.uk*

Chapter 3

international and ethnic resources

There are websites on the internet that offer links to specific record-holding bodies in countries all over the world, or at any rate to those with websites. This chapter cannot possibly list them all, so what is offered here is a selection of those likely to be of most relevance to UK researchers.

Listing by star-rating order, which is the style followed in all the other chapters, would be nonsense here, so I have had to make an admittedly rather arbitrary decision about which

national records are likely to be most useful to British users. I have assumed that they will be those in the separate countries of the British Isles and Ireland, and I have listed them first, alphabetically by country. They are preceded, however, by two websites that concentrate on records that deal specifically with London.

After the British section come those records associated with other countries or ethnic groups, again listed in alphabetical, rather than star-rating, order. The categories are, of necessity, fairly arbitrary: some sites listed cover several nationalities, whilst other countries or ethnic groups are not listed at all. If the category in which you are interested does not have its own entry here, you will need to search another website, such as The Genealogy Home Page (see p. 65), which has a link to World-Wide Genealogy Resources, or Cyndi's List (see p. 29).

England (London)

www.steeljam.dircon.co.uk
Steeljam

Overall rating: ★ ★ ★ ★			
Classification:	Records	**Readability:**	★ ★ ★ ★
Updating:	Regularly	**Content:**	★ ★ ★ ★
Navigation:	★ ★ ★ ★	**Speed:**	★ ★ ★ ★
UK			

Steve and Rita James, members of the London and North Middlesex FHS, maintain this exceptionally useful site that specialises primarily, though not exclusively, in London records. The site's usefulness is two-fold: first, it doesn't try to do too much – it concentrates specifically on London – and, second, it gives a great deal of carefully presented information about where London records are to be found and what you will find in them. Examples from the blue-lettered links on the homepage are: Churches in the City of London (many with photograph symbols alongside, which you click to enlarge; the way back is to minimise in the top right-hand corner of your browser toolbar), Lord Mayors of London and Parishes of Middlesex. Some links look further afield, for instance, the Index of County Record Offices.

SPECIAL FEATURES

Particularly useful are the three articles each starting A View of.... The three places 'viewed' are The Family Records Centre, The Guildhall Library and The London Metropolitan Archives. What is so valuable is that each gives an account of these centres from a user's point of view, literally explaining which way you turn as you walk in the main door. These accounts state what is easily found and where, what

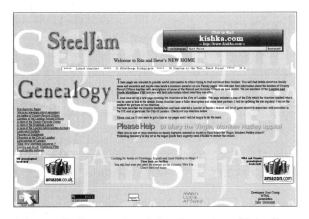

is less easily discovered, and also give such useful details as nearby restaurants or parks, and even where within the LMA you can buy pencils (which are obligatory if you are consulting their records)!

Excellent for tracking down and understanding London records – and if you are a 'virgin' researcher, the descriptions of what to expect at the three locations mentioned above is both helpful and reassuring.

www.corpoflondon.gov.uk/archives/lma

London Metropolitan Archives

Overall rating: ★ ★ ★			
Classification:	Records	**Readability:**	★ ★ ★
Updating:	Occasionally	**Content:**	★ ★ ★ ★
Navigation:	★ ★ ★	**Speed:**	★ ★

UK

The photograph collection alone contains two million images. It really is true to say that all of London life is here, from religion to the law, from schools to businesses, and from housing to hospitals.

SPECIAL FEATURES

About Us explains a little of what is contained in the collection's 31 miles of archives.

Download Free LMA Leaflets Following on from instructions for finding and using the LMA, this leads to a brief list for which you will need an Adobe Acrobat Reader, available on the spot (please refer to instructions on p. 22).

Family History Research Service links to another file for which the AAReader is required. The services of the research staff are available at a rate of £12 per half-hour, with £24 for the first hour being a minimum initial charge.

Online Visual Archive Other headings are self-explanatory, except perhaps for this one which leads to a 'New Millenium (sic) project' running from 1998 to nearly the end of 2000 to create the European Visual Archive (EVA). The object is 'access to European Heritage through digital preservation of archival collections'. Lengthy online explanations are available.

On-Line Gallery in the left-hand column on the homepage

was linked, at the time tested, to an exhibition selected from the Anglo-Jewish collections.

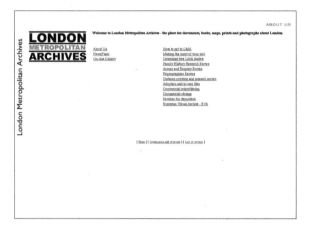

Relatively little is available for reading online here, especially if you have not downloaded a Reader, but there should still be enough to tell you whether a visit to the LMA, which is not far from the Family Records Centre (see p.31), would be worthwhile.

Ireland

www.ifhf.org
The Irish Family History Forum

Overall rating: ★★★			
Classification:	Ancestry	**Readability:**	★★★
Updating:	Occasionally	**Content:**	★★★★
Navigation:	★★★	**Speed:**	★★★★

US

Founded in 1991 by a small group of genealogical enthusiasts, the Forum is now incorporated in the US, and has connections in both Canada and England. It runs meetings, publishes a newsletter and will undertake research on behalf of individuals.

SPECIAL FEATURES

Links Because the operation of the Forum is based in New York, and all its courses take place there, this is the most useful part of the site for UK genealogists. One of these goes to The Irish at Home and Abroad, a quarterly journal that may well have articles or book reviews of interest. Selecting Irish Links from the bottom of the journal's own brown-lettered index brings up a new list, in green letters. This begins with Irish Genealogy Links and Reference Material, Online Library Catalogs in Ireland and Web Sites for Repositories of Irish Records, all of which are most valuable.

Even if you choose to ignore the North American end of the operation, with a little persistence there is still valuable material about Irish ancestry to be found here.

www.nationalarchives.ie			
The National Archives of Ireland			
Overall rating: ★ ★ ★ ★			
Classification:	Records	Readability:	★ ★ ★ ★ ★
Updating:	Regularly	Content:	★ ★ ★ ★ ★
Navigation:	★ ★ ★ ★	Speed:	★ ★ ★

IRE

The homepage explains that only relatively few of the archives can be consulted online. The object of the site is to explain what the archives contain and help you plan a visit.

SPECIAL FEATURES

About Us Start your exploration by clicking here in the small-print index at the top left of the homepage, and then select About the National Archives: Some Facts. Next, clicking on Archives Held by the National Archives explains what does still exist, given that at the beginning of the Civil War in 1922 almost all the archives held by the Public Record Office of Ireland were destroyed by fire.

Genealogy, in small letters to the top left of the homepage, leads to a page with further links to the various areas of the archival holdings. **Census Returns, Tithe Applotment** and **Primary (Griffith) Valuation, Wills and Administrations** and **Births, Marriages and Deaths** are just some of the headings.

Other links include **Genealogy Centres Listed by County** and **List of Genealogical Researchers**.

From this list, Genealogy Links will be among the most useful, offering a list of further organisations which may be of help, including the IreAtlas Townland Database, an Irish Emigrants site, Records of the Irish Constabulary and of The Valuation Office of Ireland, and many others. Another link goes to the Irish Family History Foundation at www.irishroots.net, where a county-by-county database of records can be consulted.

This densely informative website is certainly a good starting point if you have Irish connections, as it has numerous onward links, although loading may be slow.

Northern Ireland

http://proni.nics.gov.uk			
The Public Record Office of Northern Ireland			
Overall rating: ★ ★ ★ ★			
Classification: Irish records		**Readability:**	★ ★ ★ ★ ★
Updating: Regularly		**Content:**	★ ★ ★ ★ ★
Navigation: ★ ★ ★ ★ ★		**Speed:**	★ ★ ★ ★

UK

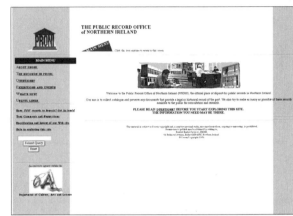

As the homepage suggests, start with Questions, where the explanation of PRONI's role is exemplary. PRONI holds both central and local government records, and certain records belonging to private individuals. Birth, Death or Marriage certificates are kept by the General Register Office, Northern Ireland (see the website of NISRA, the Northern Ireland Statistics and Research Agency, at www.nisra.gov.uk/grohome.htm, accessible from this website). The records cannot be consulted online, but there is plenty of information to help you in advance to make the most of a visit to PRONI. Remember that many Irish records were burnt in Dublin in 1922.

SPECIAL FEATURES

The Records In Proni This is a clear description of the records available, and you can find it either by selecting in the homepage index and then moving to Records Held, or at the end of the second answer given under Questions.

Census Records, Church Records, Emigration Records, Poor Law Records and **School Records** are only a few of the records held. Further down the same page, those that are particularly relevant to tracing family history are listed again, followed by those relating to local history. Clicking on

any of these takes you to extremely clear descriptions. On occasion these spread off the screen to the right, in which case you need to use the right arrow on your bottom-of-page toolbar to read them. Another link from this page leads to Academic Research and then to an interesting article on the Major Research Strengths of PRONI.

OTHER FEATURES

Other links from the homepage include **Exhibitions and Events** and **What's New**.

This thoroughly user-friendly site is well laid-out and will certainly enable you to build up a good picture of what records are held. Anyone with Irish connections should find it valuable.

Scotland

www.open.gov.uk/gros/groshome.htm
General Register Office for Scotland

Overall rating: ★ ★ ★ ★

Classification:	General	**Readability:**	★ ★ ★ ★
Updating:	Regularly	**Content:**	★ ★ ★ ★
Navigation:	★ ★ ★	**Speed:**	★ ★ ★ ★

UK

This is the longer route to the genealogical services of the General Register Office for Scotland. The direct route is via www.origins.net, but there are a few advantages to coming in this way, as you will see if you look at About GROS, below the left-of-page buttons, and then return to the buttons and select FAQ. This way you learn briefly what the function of GROS is and what you can expect its records to contain – and not contain. (Incidentally, getting the URL wrong and inputting just www.gros.org brings up a website for French fatties called 'GROS', the Groupe de Réflexion sur l'Obésité et le Surpoids, just one of those periodic amusements of trying an address without checking it first!)

SPECIAL FEATURES

Recommended offers more background under A Little History... as well as the delightful Genealogical Gems from the Old Parish Records.

Scots Origins, top button on the homepage, is probably where you will, sooner or later, head. On its dramatic lime-green background, this is the official source of genealogical data for Scotland. The Major New Announcement (May 2000) is that the Society of Genealogists (see p. 36) has selected Origins as the host for the next ten years for its own massive collection of data, adding these to the Scots records that are already provided by Origins.

Visit Scots Origins now... leads to three columns of grey boxes. Before embarking on your search here, however, please turn to the www.origins.net page in this guide (see p.44) and familiarise yourself with the payment and access system. Alternatively, click on screen on Demo and FAQ, which will give you an online explanation. GROS has, as you would expect, all the records of Births, Marriages and Deaths for Scotland, both since 1855 and, from the Old Parish Records from 1553 up to 1855.

Important records if you are tracking Scottish connections.

www.scotlandsclans.com
Scotland's Clans

Overall rating: ★ ★ ★			
Classification: Ancestry		**Readability:**	★ ★ ★
Updating: Occasionally		**Content:**	★ ★ ★
Navigation: ★ ★ ★		**Speed:**	★ ★ ★

UK

www.scotweb.co.uk
Scotweb

Overall rating: ★ ★ ★ ★			
Classification: Research		**Readability:**	★ ★ ★ ★
Updating: Regularly		**Content:**	★ ★ ★
Navigation: ★ ★ ★ ★		**Speed:**	★ ★ ★ ★

UK

Principally a site for putting in touch those researching their Scots connections.

SPECIAL FEATURES

Beginner's Guide Clicking here will only take you to a list of other suggested resources, such as the IGI, the General Register Office for Scotland and GENUKI, all obvious and already suggested in this book. The list of links under Genealogy, however, might produce a new avenue for researchers to follow.

Genealogy Detective turns out to be an American software application that you can download instantly for a sum of $24.97. It apparently comes with an unconditional money-back guarantee and two years of free future updates. Large claims are made for it, but without testing no comment can be made here.

The Top 100 Scottish Sites, accessed from a box with gold lettering to the bottom of the page, is certainly worth exploring for the onward links it then provides.

The information here is mostly fairly predictable, but the opportunity to join Scottish interest message boards or chat rooms may appeal.

Genealogists should select Clans and Tartans from the top of the homepage menu, clicking on those words rather than on the thistle logo alongside. The next page is mainly of interest to tourists, as you will see, but Scottish Roots leads to the genealogy page. You will find that it is probably too wide to fit your screen, in which case use the scroll bar at the bottom of the page to view missing text on the right.

SPECIAL FEATURES

About Scottish Roots links to an elegantly presented page (apart from the 'shadowed' text that may be less than easy to read) that explains what the research service offers, how it was set up and which records the researchers consult.

Sample Search Result, the last option in the header box, is probably the most informative in terms of helping you decide whether to use this service. Prices are found in the left-hand column, ranging from the 'Exploratory Search' to 'De Luxe Package', the latter costing nearly £500. If you worked out the cost to yourself of travelling to Scotland and staying for sufficient time to consult the records, however, this might not seem unreasonable.

A stylish site advertising a professional service for tracing Scottish ancestry.

Wales

www.celtic-connect.demon.co.uk
Celtic Connect (Welsh Ancestry)

Overall rating: ★ ★

Classification:	Research	**Readability:**	★ ★ ★
Updating:	Occasionally	**Content:**	★ ★ ★
Navigation:	★ ★	**Speed:**	★ ★ ★

UK

Recently established by two University of Wales graduates, this enterprise, based in Aberystwyth, home of the National Library of Wales, will research on your behalf. Current fees are £15 per hour, plus expenses. A feasibility study is done before you commit to any payments. You initiate this by emailing to the address in blue lettering at the bottom of the homepage text, which obtains a brochure and questionnaire. On the basis of the information you give, a report on the likely success or otherwise of the search is sent to you.

SPECIAL FEATURES

Ring of the Red Dragon This is reached by clicking on the bottom-of-the-page box which is dominated by Odin's Castle (see p. 114), while Links, at the foot of that box, leads to a number of other websites that may be of marginal interest. Here, the King Arthur/Camelot obsession is much in evidence!

This recently established a service may or may not develop in time into something useful. At present there is no means of testing the professionalism of the operation without submitting a search, but at least there is no commitment until the feasibility report is received.

www.homeusers.prestel.co.uk/TYHAFREN/census.htm
Wyndham's Pages

Overall rating: ★ ★ ★

Classification:	Ancestry	**Readability:**	★ ★ ★
Updating:	Occasionally	**Content:**	★ ★ ★
Navigation:	★ ★ ★	**Speed:**	★ ★ ★

UK

The most useful part of this personal website is the information under 1881 Wales Census, last on the index on the homepage.

SPECIAL FEATURES

1881 Wales Census Clicking here leads to the offer of a free look-up service to those researching, in particular, their Welsh ancestry. The 1881 Census is the most complete, but as the indexes that begin lower down the page show, records actually start with fragmentary details from the 1841 Census. Researchers are reminded that Census details are arranged by surname, not by address.

If tracing your Welsh connections is proving difficult, this may be a good place to look for help.

OTHER SITES OF INTEREST

All Irish Clans and Names
www.clansandnames.org

The Irish Family History Foundation
www.irishroots.net

Irish Genealogical Congress
www.ancestordetective.com/IGC.htm

The Ulster Historical Foundation
www.irishroots.net/AntmDown.htm

Northern Ireland Family History Society (associated with the Federation of Family History Societies, see p. 33)
www.nifhs.org

Genfindit
www.genfindit.com

Genfindit is a service for ordering online copies of Scottish and Irish Vital Records. Payment is required so the system has not been actively tested, though the online testimonials from users read encouragingly.

International

www.genealogylinks.net
Genealogylinks.net

Overall rating: ★ ★ ★ ★			
Classification:	Records	**Readability:**	★ ★ ★ ★
Updating:	Regularly	**Content:**	★ ★ ★ ★
Navigation:	★ ★	**Speed:**	★ ★

US

This index of genealogy sites, containing numerous internal links, is very clearly 'catalogued', which makes using it a pleasure. On the homepage are two contents lists, the one on the left indicating what is in the databases, under International, UK & Ireland, Europe, United States, Canada, Australia & NZ and Ships Passenger Lists; the one on the right offering What's New, Top 10 Homepages, Your Own Homepage, Genealogy Books and other Links.

SPECIAL FEATURES

Cemeteries, Censuses, Military and **Ships** Apart from a few general entries at the beginning of each one, the various national sections are each subdivided into these categories. Looking at County Durham under the UK & Ireland section, however, produced nothing for Cemeteries or Censuses, and for Military only lists of casualties from the two World Wars in Ryton and West Rainton – so, as ever, the site is only as good as the material that has been put into it. Similarly, Spain and Greece, tested in the Europe section, had only a handful of general entries each and nothing under the four headings above.

United States Clicking here, however, you will find that the lists are far more complete, with both Canada and Australia

& NZ not far behind. On one occasion tested a great many of the subsequent links were not opening up, which explains the low star-rating under 'Navigation' above. On a later visit, things were working better. This unevenness is presumably not normally the case and is just an indication of the periodic frustrations of using the internet. Those links that did open were helpful, though in the UK cases they normally led to GENUKI (see p. 34).

The clarity of layout at this website would make it a very attractive one to use, assuming it was up and running properly. However, I have no reason to believe that this is not normally the case.

www.worldgenweb.org
The WorldGenWeb Project

Overall rating: ★ ★			
Classification:	Records	**Readability:**	★ ★ ★
Updating:	Occasionally	**Content:**	★ ★
Navigation:	★ ★ ★	**Speed:**	★ ★

(INT)

This is a volunteer-run organisation, launched in 1996, whose mission is to deliver genealogical information free of charge to researchers in any country of the world. Now hosted by RootsWeb (see p. 71), the idea is that each country's databank should be staffed by people who either live in or are familiar with that country's research resources. The result is only as good as the volunteers who contribute, and that, for the time being, is the problem. The homepage scrolls down to a map indicating that the only unaffiliated countries are Canada and the US, although their records are also made available.

SPECIAL FEATURES

UKGenWeb Archives Although this is an admirable project in principle, on the tested date the amount of information available on this part of the site was minimal.

MediterraneanGenWeb Archives The only entry here was 'Buriels' (sic) in the American section of the Protestant Cemetery in 'Instanbul (sic), Turkey'.

CaribbeanGenWeb Archives It rapidly becomes evident that the West Indies is the only area to be remotely well covered, and here you'll find a worthwhile list of records, such as the emigration lists for Bermuda or Jamaica, baptismal records in Antigua, or records of the Wesleyan Methodist Church or the Society of Friends (Quakers) in the British Virgin Islands.

OTHER FEATURES

Incidentally, the Germany GenWeb Project's website within the WorldGenWeb, which can be found at www.rootsweb.com/~wggerman/index.htm, has recently been voted the best site on the Web by the readers of Eastman's Online Genealogy Newsletter (see p. 136), though a quick visit did not immediately indicate why that website would be so much further ahead of any others.

Probably only worth a look at present if you have Caribbean connections, thought this is one to watch for the future in the hope that it will eventually build into something really valuable.

Australia

www.cohsoft.com.au/afhc
The Australian Family History Compendium

Overall rating: ★ ★ ★ ★			
Classification:	Records	**Readability:**	★ ★ ★ ★ ★
Updating:	Regularly	**Content:**	★ ★ ★ ★
Navigation:	★ ★ ★ ★ ★	**Speed:**	★ ★ ★ ★ ★

This well-organised and rapid website is devoted to the exploration of Australian records, along with much other information about how to set about genealogical research both in Australia and elsewhere.

SPECIAL FEATURES

The homepage is clearly set out under such headings as Beginners; Education, Courses and Tutorials; Demographics and Population; Heraldry; History, and so on.

AFHC Guide This comes about a third of the way down the homepage, and is a link to the list of actual records that are available online. Each of these has its own link, in blue lettering.

This clear, general-purpose website is probably the best entry point for anyone seeking information about ancestors in Australia.

www.alphalink.com.au/~aigs

Australian Institute of Genealogical Studies Inc.

Overall rating: ★ ★ ★ ★			
Classification:	Records	**Readability:**	★ ★ ★ ★
Updating:	Regularly	**Content:**	★ ★ ★
Navigation:	★ ★ ★	**Speed:**	★ ★ ★ ★

(AUS)

This well-laid-out website is almost unobtrusive in its presentation. It proves to be a mine of information about Australian and associated records.

SPECIAL FEATURES

The brown links on the homepage offer such categories as Library, Catalogue, Research Services, The Genealogist's Journal and Bookshop, all of which are self-explanatory.

Genealogy Links contains some very useful material, including some searchable indexes, such as Irish Convicts Transported to Australia and Index to Certificates of Freedom 1823–69 of Convicts Transported to Australia. Many of these links go on to other websites, mostly Australian in origin. Those links tested were working well and the onward material on offer was impressive.

A valuable website for anyone exploring Australian connections, particularly those interested in searching the convict transportation records.

www.shipping.cohsoft.com.au/cgi-bin/db/ship.pl

Public Record Office - Victoria's Archives

Overall rating: ★ ★ ★			
Classification:	Immigrants	**Readability:**	★ ★ ★ ★
Updating:	Occasionally	**Content:**	★ ★ ★
Navigation:	★ ★ ★	**Speed:**	★ ★ ★ ★

(AUS)

This is a straightforward search facility, listing immigrants arriving at the Australian port of Victoria in 1852–1879, from British and foreign ports.

The more information you give, the more likely you are to find the relevant match, but even scanty details may be enough. The homepage explains how to fill in the search boxes. A successful search will lead to a fiche number and page number, which can then be ordered.

SPECIAL FEATURES

Just above the search boxes is an **About** link, which leads to a page that is probably worth reading first. At the bottom of that page, **Macbeth Genealogical Services** is a further useful link.

Narrowly specific in its remit, this is nevertheless a useful point from which to track down an emigrant to Australia known to have landed in Victoria between the given dates.

Canada

www.archives.ca
National Archives of Canada

Overall rating: ★ ★ ★			
Classification:	Records	**Readability:**	★ ★ ★
Updating:	Occasionally	**Content:**	★ ★ ★ ★
Navigation:	★ ★ ★	**Speed:**	★ ★ ★

(CAN)

The dual logo on the homepage (in French and English, this being Canadian) offers no links and the only way into this website appears to be to click on either the word English or French in very small letters underneath. The link **About the NA** is not especially informative.

SPECIAL FEATURES

Online Research Tool: Archivia Net or Services to the Public
By selecting either of these you will get a bit more information, although it is not easy to start searching Archivia until you know what sort of material the records contain.

Probably the best advice is to start by clicking on Publications. This leads to a list that includes Tracing your Ancestors in Canada, a publication that can either be ordered online to be sent to you or can be downloaded with the help of an Adobe Acrobat Reader (see p.22).

OTHER FEATURES

There is also a link, from the homepage or from the previously-mentioned list to the **National Library of Canada**. Once there, click once again on **English** to enter the website, and then on **Services for Researchers**. You will be offered a search box, into which you can input the single word **Genealogy**. This brought up a very good list of publications held by the Library. If there is a shorter route to this point, it was not immediately evident.

Good information about Canadian records is certainly stored here, though it doesn't seem to be the easiest of websites to navigate.

www.cadvision.com/traces
Traces

Overall rating: ★ ★ ★			
Classification: Records	Readability:	★ ★ ★	
Updating: Occasionally	Content:	★ ★ ★	
Navigation: ★ ★ ★	Speed:	★ ★ ★	

CAN

The homepage of this Canadian website looks somewhat alarming, with its black background and futuristic silver cones at the top of the page. You feel you might be about to meet Darth Vader around the next corner. What this has to do with Canadian records is not clear, but the site proves worth investigation.

SPECIAL FEATURES

From the two possibilities on the homepage select **Traces From Your Past**. This immediately transports you to a list headed **British Strays in Canada** and then **British Residents with Canadian Connections**. Admittedly, this is mainly a route to tracing present-day connections, rather than ones from the past, but it may still prove helpful.

Further down the same list **Some Canadian and UK Research Links** moves you to a quite different page, this time bordered down both sides with maple leaves. Here you get into the meat of the website from a British researcher's point of view.

An odd site, as well as a personal one, but it rewards investigation.

Europe

www.eegsociety.org
East European Genealogical Society

Overall rating: ★ ★ ★			
Classification: Records	Readability:	★ ★ ★ ★	
Updating: Regularly	Content:	★ ★ ★	
Navigation: ★ ★ ★	Speed:	★ ★ ★	

CAN

If all you know is a surname or the name of a village, this would probably be the best place to start trying to find out more about your East European connections.

SPECIAL FEATURES

It is worth reading the homepage before going further. Thereafter, the Database Search or the Surname/Village Index are the two areas in which you can look for your name or village.

Back Issues links to the Journal of the Society of Eastern European Genealogists. The contents of recent issues are well listed, and the Back Issues Order Form is at the bottom of the page.

A good starting point for those trying to trace East European connections.

Germany

www.germanmigration.com
German Migration Resource Center

Overall rating: ★ ★ ★			
Classification: Records		**Readability:**	★ ★ ★ ★
Updating: Occasionally		**Content:**	★ ★ ★ ★
Navigation: ★ ★ ★ ★		**Speed:**	★ ★

US

If there are German ancestors in your family tree, you will certainly want to visit this website. Moving around it can be rather slow and, even when you have found what you want, you will need to subscribe, though you can choose to do so for a period as short as one month.

SPECIAL FEATURES

Top Five Queries gives you an idea of the sort of queries that are posted here. To read the whole list you must subscribe.

Books gives an exceptionally good list of books, divided under Genealogy References and Migration Resources.

Links leads to numerous additional websites under useful category headings. Among these are History and Culture, Language and Handwriting (which includes books, software, a glossary of German words used in official manuscripts and Sample Letters in German), Migration Research and Links to Major German Sites such as www.germanroots.com.

See also p. 58 for more about the Germany GenWeb Project.

An invaluable starting point if you have German connections.

Jamaica

www.jamaicanfamilysearch.com
Jamaican Family Search - Genealogy Research Library

Overall rating: ★ ★ ★			
Classification: Records		**Readability:**	★ ★ ★ ★
Updating: Occasionally		**Content:**	★ ★ ★
Navigation: ★ ★ ★ ★		**Speed:**	★ ★ ★ ★

US

An all-purpose genealogy site for those with Jamaican ancestry.

SPECIAL FEATURES

Jamaica Almanac, on the homepage, explains that these records are the approximate equivalent of census returns for Jamaica, starting in 1810. There are also details of Civil Lists, Military Lists, Monumental Inscriptions of the British West Indies and Jamaican Registers and Wills. It is not until you get towards the bottom of the page that the actual links become available. These take you to 'samples only'; access to the detailed records is by subscription, currently ranging from $4 for a week's access to $40 for six months.

Surname List brings up a short list of surnames (currently fewer than 20) that individuals are researching, with email contact details. The last of the blue links, Announcements and Useful Links, leads to another dozen websites but most of these purvey contemporary information about Jamaica rather than historical.

Those with Jamaican connections will find this a useful starting point.

Jewish

www.ort.org/jgsgb
The Jewish Genealogical Society of Great Britain

Overall rating: ★ ★ ★ ★

Classification:	Records	Readability:	★★★★
Updating:	Regularly	Content:	★★★★
Navigation:	★★★★	Speed:	★★★★

UK

Trying to find Jewish connections is greatly helped by coming here first, as it automatically reduces the size of the databases being searched. A lot of the material is submitted by members, but there are also other valuable records available for online consultation.

SPECIAL FEATURES

The JGSGB Index of Marriages, recorded at the Princelet (Princes) Street Synagogue in Spitalfields, London, from 1897–1907, can be viewed via the bride's or the bridegroom's surname. Another link from the homepage goes to the London Jewish Chronicle death announcements from 1995–1998, while earlier announcements (from 1790 onwards) are to be found under Anglo-Jewish Miscellanies further down the same page.

Cemetery Records Index Page is another recently completed page, allowing search by surname of the burials at the two Jewish cemeteries at Cheshunt and Enfield.

Names in Books is an ongoing project to database books in which Jewish names are recorded.

Photograph Gallery is a project to assemble a collection of photographs of places of interest (not of people or families) for Jewish genealogists.

Shemot, the Journal of the JGSGB, can't be read online, though a list of the contents of recent issues is available and it can be ordered via email. For this, click on Publications, where you will also find A Beginner's Guide to Jewish Genealogy in Great Britain, which can be ordered online.

Family Finder Index leads to a search service that can either be downloaded in its entirety or, if you are a member, be accessed via email.

An indispensable site for those with Jewish connections, well set out and easily used.

JewishGen Inc.

www.jewishgen.org

This American-based volunteer organisation is dedicated to helping people of Jewish origin trace their ancestry.

Netherlands

www.cbg.nl/english/main.htm
Centraal Bureau voor Genealogie

Overall rating: ★ ★ ★ ★			
Classification:	Records	**Readability:**	★ ★ ★ ★
Updating:	Occasionally	**Content:**	★ ★ ★
Navigation:	★ ★ ★ ★	**Speed:**	★ ★ ★ ★

NE

This is the principal website for tracing Dutch connections, and it also gives access to the collections of the Royal Dutch Society for Genealogy and Heraldry.

SPECIAL FEATURES

Collections is the link on which to click to get information about the records that are available here. Everything is well organised and the English version of the website is excellent. Other useful links are Heraldry and Research.

Genealogy Discussion, which looks promising, was actually still under construction at the date tested.

Online Research Guide leads to a further link, entitled How to Start Searching for Dutch Ancestors, a clear and helpful article that can be read online. Other possibly useful titles are **Primary Genealogical Records in the Netherlands** and **Heraldry**.

Links transports you to a long, well-organised list of further websites you may wish to consult. Those tested were working well.

This is the best place to start if you are seeking information about ancestors or connections in the Netherlands.

North America

www.genhomepage.com
The Genealogy Home Page

Overall rating: ★ ★ ★ ★ ★			
Classification:	Immigration	**Readability:**	★ ★ ★ ★ ★
Updating:	Regularly	**Content:**	★ ★ ★ ★
Navigation:	★ ★ ★ ★ ★	**Speed:**	★ ★ ★ ★ ★

(US)

Sponsored by Family Tree Maker Online, this American site is most valuable for its function as an index of websites, particularly those devoted to North American records. It also lists a huge number of other websites worth consulting.

SPECIAL FEATURES

North American Genealogy Resources is a very helpful link that leads to a vast directory of relevant websites, starting with Canada, Mexico and the US in general, and moving on to more specialist information sources.

World-Wide Genealogy Resources is similarly well organised, listing genealogical resources alphabetically by country. Some of the sites listed, of course, are in the languages of the countries concerned.

Religious Genealogy Resources, Libraries and **Maps, Geography, Deeds and Photography** are other useful links from the homepage.

With genealogical and family history research having now reached obsession levels in the US, a site of this kind, which collects all the relevant websites in one place and indexes them logically, is particularly welcome.

www.ellisisland.org
The Statue of Liberty - Ellis Island Foundation Inc.

Overall rating: ★ ★ ★			
Classification:	Immigration	**Readability:**	★ ★ ★ ★
Updating:	Occasionally	**Content:**	★ ★ ★ ★
Navigation:	★ ★ ★	**Speed:**	★ ★ ★

(US)

The resources of the Ellis Island Foundation are detailed here, their function being to record details of American immigration. More than 17 million people were processed at Ellis Island, the registration centre for the Port of New York, between 1892 and 1924, the largest human migration in modern history.

SPECIAL FEATURES

Immigration Museum introduces the commemorative displays at the Museum, in the Ellis Island buildings close to the Statue of Liberty. The Highlights of the Museum are described, followed by Visitation (sic) Information.

The American Family Immigration History Center is currently working to put its records online, a resource that will be extremely useful once completed. You can support this venture by becoming a Charter Founder, a link to which is given at the bottom of the page.

Widely recognised as a remarkable record of immigrants to America from the late 19th-century onwards, this will be a really valuable resource once the actual data can be read online.

Romany

http://website.lineone.net/~rtfhs
Romany & Traveller Family History Society

Overall rating: ★ ★ ★ ★			
Classification: Records		**Readability:**	★ ★ ★ ★
Updating: Occasionally		**Content:**	★ ★ ★
Navigation: ★ ★ ★ ★		**Speed:**	★ ★ ★ ★

UK

This clear, straightforwardly presented site is the place to come if you have Romany, traveller or gypsy connections.

SPECIAL FEATURES

Was your Ancestor a Gypsy? is a good general introduction to the subject.

Publications contains a detailed list of books and transcriptions, each with brief details of contents.

Romany Routes is the Society's Journal. Clicking here leads to indexes of the surnames that appear in each of the recent issues.

Links to Other Sites is what it says, with a useful list of other websites from which to explore the history of the Romany lifestyle.

The best starting point if you need to trace ancestors who may have been gypsies.

OTHER SITES OF INTEREST

The Circus, Theatre and Music Hall Families Page
www.users.globalnet.co.uk/~paulln/circus.htm

This site is worth consulting if you need information about Romany/Gypsy connections. It also offers the opportunity to subscribe to the online message archive 'Itinerant Roots'.

West Indies

http://ourworld.compuserve.com/homepages/vroyal
West Indies Surname Interests Lists

Overall rating: ★ ★ ★			
Classification: Records		**Readability:**	★ ★ ★
Updating: Occasionally		**Content:**	★ ★
Navigation: ★ ★ ★		**Speed:**	★ ★ ★

US

Compiled by Vaughn W. Royal in Virginia, this is a means of putting in touch those who are already researching individual West Indies surnames, which are listed alphabetically island by island, with those seeking information. Contact is by email, and both subscribing and submitting names are free.

SPECIAL FEATURES

Download Latest Issue as a Text File or as a Zip File allows you to view the list, with contact information for researchers at the end of the document. You are warned that the document in its entirety is more than 100 pages long. If you know where you are searching, the next link permits a shortcut to a country-by-country list, giving only those names being researched in that country, with email contact details given alongside each name.

Worth taking a chance here, as you may well come across someone researching the very name you are seeking.

Chapter 4

searching for names

By all means head immediately for a website that offers a name-search facility, type in the name you are interested in and hope for a result. Don't necessarily assume, however, that this is the best way of getting helpful information. One reason is that the majority of websites offering this facility are based in the United States, and although there are many families in this country with relatives across the Atlantic, there are still many more who have no American connections whatsoever. Nobody in the US is, therefore,

likely to be researching those names, unless perhaps they are pursuing a lateral rather than a vertical (father-to-father) search. As the information contributed to name-search sites is mostly volunteered by individuals, you see the problem.

First of all, it is important to understand the difference between one-name studies and personal family trees, which are usually available online in GEDCOM (GEnealogical Data COMmunication) form.

One-name studies, correctly defined, seek all occurrences, past and present, of a single surname, anywhere in the world, as opposed to tracing a specific family tree within that name. More often than not, they are most useful to the private researcher as a means of eliminating the inclusion of 'wrong' ancestors or branches of the family tree. You may, however, become fascinated by the wider aspects of the search, such as the geographical migration of the name or its persistence within certain professions, and wish to launch a one-name study of your own. If so, you can register with the Guild of One-Name Studies (GOONS, see p. 75), on the understanding that you will undertake to collect all references worldwide, not restricted by family or locality, and that you will personally deal with all reply-paid enquiries sent to you.

As a user of one-name studies websites, be warned that each site will only be as good as the person/people who contribute to it, so you may find that they are disorganised, that a lot of information is repeated rather than consolidated, and that response times are slow. Depending on the contributors, they may also, of course, be inaccurate. Moreover, because one-name studies sites assemble information on a global scale, they are likely to become enormous unless they are dealing with an unusual surname. Having offered those warnings, however, it may turn out that you find exactly the site, names and personal contacts you need and your researches will accordingly take a huge leap forward. Certainly, they're worth a try.

In addition to one-name sites, thousands of individuals have by now posted their own personal family trees on the web. They are also well worth exploring, especially those posted here in the UK, in case you find that someone else is researching the same branch of a family tree as you and is perhaps further along with their research. Allowing for the need to check the connections they have made (and good researchers will always document their sources), a lucky encounter of this sort could prove to be a shortcut to filling in a whole area of your own pedigree.

Alternatively, if you have already done lots of work yourself and have files of well-documented genealogical information about your own ancestors, you may want to post your own family tree on the web. You don't have to set up an independent website to do this. There are several website-hosting services that specialise in genealogy, not all requiring a subscription but usually needing to receive your file in GEDCOM form. There are websites here that tell you how to create your own GEDCOM.

Finally, you may want to interact online with other enthusiasts. Again, simply explore the websites in this section and you will find plenty of mailing lists, message boards or individual email contacts with whom you can communicate, both asking and answering questions, sharing information and generally enjoying the whole field of ancestral research.

Briefly, mailing lists focus on individual topics and any message you email to such a list will get distributed to all members of the group. Conversely, you will receive every message any other member of the group posts, so it may be worth looking at the archived messages, if the list has such a facility, before deciding whether to join or not. Newsgroups are similar to mailing lists, in that they also focus on special topics or areas. To join most newsgroups you will need a newsreader, probably downloadable from the web. Deja News, however, is accessible to all (see p. 142).

www.rootsweb.com

RootsWeb.com

Overall rating: ★ ★ ★ ★			
Classification: General		**Readability:**	★ ★ ★ ★
Updating: Occasionally		**Content:**	★ ★ ★
Navigation: ★ ★ ★ ★		**Speed:**	★ ★ ★ ★

US

This is the internet's oldest and largest free genealogy site. The homepage immediately offers two search facilities, where you can search either by name or by keywords, such as a location or a topic. Below this, however, is probably the best place to start. Here there are about 100 preliminary links under the headings **Getting Started, Research Templates, Major Search Engines, Mailing Lists - Genealogy Only, Message Boards (GenConnect), Web Sites - Genealogy Only, Other Tools/Resources, Famous and Infamous, Hosted Volunteer Genealogy Projects** (including such things as transcribing the names of passengers on immigrant ships or recording the inscriptions on tombstones), **Help** (including Frequently Asked Questions), **Buy or Sell, Contributing to Rootsweb, About Us** and **Communities at Rootsweb**. Some of these pages are still under construction.

SPECIAL FEATURES

Returning to the original 'Search' facility, enter the name(s) required and press return on the keyboard to proceed. Searching by name will produce a list of results, which, in the case tested, gave over 50 links under **Surname Helper** for the surname on its own, though none for the requested complete name. Other additional entries appeared under such headings as **Obit Times, GenSeeker, US Gen Web Archives** and **Arkansas GLO Records**. This should be sufficient to indicate that the online material here is again predominantly American, which is one reason for its overall star-rating above. In the test case, however, pursuing the Surname Helper route led to a list of locations, some of which were in the UK, or family associations. Following up the most likely UK location then produced a further list of nearly 20 recently posted requests for information and answers, which read as a virtual conversation if opened sequentially.

Hosted Volunteer Genealogy Projects offers, near the top of a long list, FreeBMD, a project that will in due course be of enormous interest to UK users, as it plans to provide free online access to all the births, marriages and deaths recorded under the Civil Registration index since 1837. Of the 100 million entries up to 1900, volunteers have so far only transcribed fewer than two million, so there is a very long way to go, but this is definitely one to watch.

Famous and Infamous offers Notable Kin, Royal and Noble Lineages (currently featuring the ancestry of Camilla Parker-Bowles) and US Presidential Ancestor Tables, all presented in a somewhat tongue-in-cheek style, though serious in terms of research.

The commitment of RootsWeb to a completely free service deserves wholehearted support. Urgent requests for voluntary contributions to support the site are periodically flagged up. FreeBMD is certainly very exciting, while for tracking down members of a family known to have emigrated to the US RootsWeb would certainly be a first point of call, and following the Surname Helper route described above might well lead back to the UK via an interesting new contact.

www.ancestry.com
Ancestry.com

Overall rating: ★ ★ ★			
Classification: General		**Readability:**	★ ★
Updating: Occasionally		**Content:**	★ ★
Navigation: ★ ★		**Speed:**	★ ★ ★

US

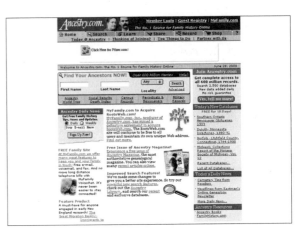

The busy, cluttered homepage is off-putting. When most recently visited it was advertising everything from the chance to win a 'Trip to Your Homeland' in the Ancestry World Tree Sweepstakes (complete with two exclamation marks), a sign-up box to receive 'Ancestry Daily News', another sign-up to become a member of Ancestry.com, a link to lots of 'FREE' message boards, a list of Today's New Databases, a link to Ancestry Resources, a feature on Jewish genealogy and even the opportunity to read the history of the White House Easter Egg Roll and the text of the Haggadah for Passover! Meanwhile, there was still room to squeeze in some clip-art pictures. At the top of the page, however, under the flashing banner headline that says you can search 550 million names for less than $5 a month, is a search box headed Find Your Ancestors NOW! Instead of panicking, try starting there.

SPECIAL FEATURES

Search lets you put in a first and second name, or simply a surname, specify a locality or not as you choose, and then press the search button. Tested with one reasonably unusual surname, it produced 94 Ancestry World Tree entries, 208 Social Security Death Index entries, 211 current US Telephone and Address Listings, and links to message boards and that name's 'Surname Community'. The search also produced hits in a number of other categories, such as

Census records, military records, periodicals, newspapers and so on. Using the 'back' button and then refining the search by adding a first name, the number of hits was drastically reduced, to two current telephone/address listings, the message boards and the **Surname Community** (which proved to have the 94 entries). One hit in each case was apparently available in **Vital & Church Records** and **Biography & History**, but this was as far as it was possible to go without paying.

Learn introduces various family history resources, principally the Ancestry Library, which could be useful.

Share is really the means whereby the whole site is compiled, namely by individuals posting their personal information on the message boards, contributing to the Ancestry World Tree or joining the Research Registry. This is where the possibility for unreliable information is inevitably introduced.

Record offers online website space for your family tree and a means of staying in touch with your family worldwide.

Shop takes you to publications, software packages and

other products of interest to researchers, all for sale at the click of a button, and gives you the opportunity to sign up for the ProductWatch newsletter. Be aware that using this US-based facility will probably mean incurring import taxes and will certainly involve carriage costs.

The question-mark that comes at the end of the card-index tabs offers help via Customer Support (as they say, 'NOT a toll-free call') and also, as its last item, give answers to FAQs. This, however, only answers questions about subscribing.

FamilyHistory.com and MyFamily.com are both associated websites, which are accessible from within this website.

This site is likely to be of relatively little use to UK users unless you already know that you have family members in the US but don't know how to find them. The onward links, however, are numerous and will probably reward exploration.

www.gendex.com
GENDEX

Overall rating: ★ ★ ★			
Classification:	Name-search	Readability:	★★★★
Updating:	Occasionally	Content:	★★★
Navigation:	★★★★	Speed:	★★★

US

GENDEX is an American website, run by Gene Stark. It calls itself 'an enterprise devoted to advancing the progress of family history and genealogy research on the World Wide Web'.

It offers three main services: a GEDCOM to HTML translator called GED2HTML, the GENDEX-WWW Genealogical Index containing over 12 million names, which can be searched online, and Genealogical web page storage, which can be rented for a 'modest' fee. It would have obtained a higher overall star-rating had it not been for its probably limited use to UK users.

SPECIAL FEATURES

GENDEX-WWW Genealogical Index This is likely to be the most useful feature on the site. Clicking on Access the Index leads to three possibilities, of which the first is the surname index. This, in turn, leads to a clear two-box submission form, which asks for either 'a prefix of a surname' or an actual surname and search for 'soundex-equivalents', that is surnames that are pronounced in the same way but are not necessarily spelt the same.

Also offered is an index of individuals who don't actually have a surname, as well as a list of surnames 'beginning with characters outside the range A–Z'. The surname tested immediately produced some of the right information, though nothing new, probably because, once again, it works from a US-based starting point.

Although American, this site is simple, clear and uncluttered, so hunting American connections could be quickly tried and dismissed, if not helpful.

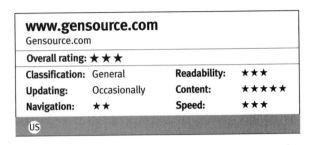

www.gensource.com
Gensource.com

Overall rating: ★★★			
Classification:	General	**Readability:**	★★★
Updating:	Occasionally	**Content:**	★★★★★
Navigation:	★★	**Speed:**	★★★

US

Set up by Deb Kinneer, Gensource contains three major databases, collating a large number of genealogy websites submitted by individual genealogists. For this reason the homepage ends with an accuracy disclaimer. The majority of the records are US-based.

SPECIAL FEATURES

Common Threads has the object of putting individuals researching the same family name (surname) in touch with each other. It is aimed particularly at helping those who have reached a 'dead end' in their researches, and is

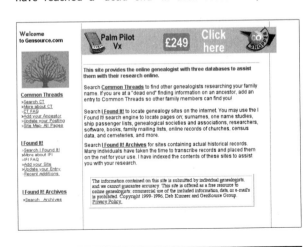

certainly not intended as a forum for people to post their entire family trees. Good information about the service, which is free, is found in the left-of-page index under More about CT and CT FAQ. It is worth noting that, when you input the name of the person you are searching for, you should use 'and' to link the parts of the name (for instance, 'John and Henry and Smith'), otherwise the search will produce every John, every Henry and every Smith.

I Found it! is a database of genealogy websites in many different categories, as explained on the homepage. A brief test suggested that keeping the search simple would be necessary. For example, inputting simply 'occupations' brought up a useful short list of references, including a link to glossaries under www.genealogy-quest.com.

I Found it! Archives, meanwhile, is a growing list of actual archives that have been transcribed onto the internet by individuals and can, consequently, be consulted online. This, of course, means that the selection of what is available is quite random, according to where the personal interests of the people doing the transcribing happen to lie.

If you have really run into a brick wall in your research, this would certainly be one place to flag up your difficulty in the hope that some other individual might be able to help out.

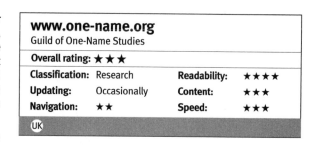

www.one-name.org
Guild of One-Name Studies

Overall rating: ★ ★ ★			
Classification:	Research	**Readability:**	★ ★ ★ ★
Updating:	Occasionally	**Content:**	★ ★ ★
Navigation:	★ ★	**Speed:**	★ ★ ★

UK

For anyone interested in following up research through a one-name studies website, GOONS will be the best place to start, precisely because it is UK-based. Note that a one-name study seeks to research all occurrences of a single surname, not to follow a particular family tree. Note also that the only method of return to the homepage, or indeed any other, is the 'back' button on the top toolbar.

SPECIAL FEATURES

Services Available to Members explains that The Guild Email Forum, free permanent email addresses and access to the

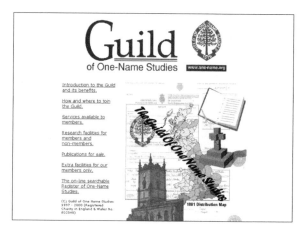

Biography Database 1680–1830 are all restricted to members.

Research Facilities for Members and Non-Members explains how requesting help from Guild Members, who all give their services voluntarily, is made easier if you ask specific rather than general questions and are patient about response times. Links to Other Websites will also be found on this page and includes links to websites such as GENUKI, The Federation of Family History Societies, Cyndi's List, Gen-Link UK, The Society of Genealogists and the Scottish and Welsh Associations of Family History Societies.

Given that there is nowhere near enough space in this book to list one-name sites individually, your best route to exploring whether there is anything in them for you is probably to start here. That way you can take advantage of the good explanation of what one-name sites are and how to contribute. It probably makes sense to do a quick search and then use Cyndi's List if you want to try further afield.

www.kindredkonnections.com
Kindred Konnections

Overall rating: ★ ★ ★			
Classification:	Name-search	**Readability:**	★ ★ ★ ★
Updating:	Occasionally	**Content:**	★ ★ ★
Navigation:	★ ★ ★	**Speed:**	★ ★

US

Claiming to be one of the most advanced genealogical research sites in the world, this is the online presence of the Family History Research Center in Utah (but don't mistake this for the IGI/Mormon index). It does not appear to be always possible to download pages and then work offline, so you may prefer to print out some of the basic information offered in the left-hand column before getting too involved. Current subscription rates are $5 for ten days, rising to $100 per year, with a one-off offer of a free month if you submit a GEDCOM file of your own family history containing at least 15 families and 60 individuals. Click on Free Hour or Month, however, and you can have a trial run for an hour before registering. Incidentally, this big, stylish site may prove slightly too wide for your screen; by scrolling right or left at the bottom of the page, however, you can probably adjust it to the point where you can see everything you need to see.

SPECIAL FEATURES

Free Services offers a Demo Room, which may be a useful way of exploring the possibilities of the site, while FAQs will be found under About This Site. Yet again, the information available is dependent on what individuals have submitted. So, the 1871 Cornwall, UK, Census, for instance, happens to be available because someone has put it there, but there is apparently little other UK information.

How to Contact Us is valuable not so much for the contact

details as for what follows further down the page: a brilliantly clear article headed What is a GEDCOM File? This has to be about the simplest description of what GEDCOM means and how you use it anywhere on the Net. It alone would make the site worth visiting.

Site Map is not in any sense a map but a list of services which, at the bottom of the page, offers Other Web Sites.

If looking for UK information, you will be better off starting with a UK-based equivalent, like GENUKI. But as soon as you find links in the US or elsewhere to chase up, this is probably the next best step. Don't miss the GEDCOM link, anyway.

www.ukbdmexchange.org.uk
The UK BDM (Births, Deaths and Marriages) Exchange

Overall rating: ★ ★ ★			
Classification: Name-search		**Readability:**	★★★★
Updating: Regularly		**Content:**	★★★
Navigation: ★★★		**Speed:**	★★★

UK

On the occasions tested, this website was unusually slow, perhaps because of the large amount of data it contains. It is a free resource, putting you in touch with other genealogists and listing the BDM certificates they hold. To understand the object of the service, it is essential to click first on Help in the purple buttons to the left of the homepage. If this button is not immediately on view (it is near the bottom of the list), scroll down on the adjacent bar. The page that now comes up is headed How to Navigate the UK BDM Exchange. Before navigating, however, you still need to understand what the site is trying to do. Click on About in blue lettering at the bottom of the page, and at last you get answers. This difficulty of introduction and the slow response times account for the relatively low overall star-rating, but the idea itself is brilliant.

SPECIAL FEATURES

Use the purple buttons down the left-hand-side of the page to select from a list including **Births, Deaths** and **ParMarr** (Parish Marriages), and then click on the relevant letter of the alphabet from the bar along the bottom of the page to see if anyone is researching the name you are interested in. If you know a maiden, but not a married, name, click on **Wives**, which may produce the married name you need, in which case return to one of the earlier lists.

If you find a record you want to consult further, contact the researcher at the address indicated. Those certificates that have proved irrelevant or are no longer wanted have a 'Y' beside them, meaning that the researcher in question is prepared to pass them on. Researchers will still give information, of course, even where the actual certificates are being retained, so if you have any certificates of your own that you are prepared to share or pass on, register here!

This service, set up in 1997, is an excellent idea and a very necessary one. It is already slow, and risks getting slower as more and more data is entered, which is a problem that will have to be solved. However, the work done by Graham Pitt, who runs the site, is admirable.

www.infokey.com
Family History Archive Library

Overall rating: ★ ★			
Classification:	Entertainment	**Readability:**	★ ★ ★ ★
Updating:	Occasionally	**Content:**	★
Navigation:	★ ★ ★	**Speed:**	★ ★ ★ ★

CAN

Be very wary of this and other similar sites. The giftware on offer is amusing and harmless enough, but this sort of website can easily mislead.

SPECIAL FEATURES

Headed 'Flip Through the Pages of History and trace your Family Name' ('flip' being the operative word), the homepage invites you immediately to search for your family name. Areas in which to search are **Family Histories, Tartans and Clans, Coat of Arms, Castles & Palaces, Ancient Genealogies, Family Mottos, Family Crests** and a **Combined Search**. These are not available as links from the list on the right of the page, but only by clicking and selecting from the right-hand box headed 'Select Index'.

Each one, of course, leads to the offer to sell you, for a considerable sum, a Family History Scroll ('A Masterpiece!' and 'individually researched with the utmost precision') or your coat of arms on everything from mugs and plates to mouse pads and golfing shirts.

The dangerous aspect of all this is that inexperienced researchers can be misled into believing, as indeed they are told here, that meticulous professionals have undertaken the search on their behalf. In fact, the results of any search will be highly generalised and, unless you have a surname so rare that there is only one line, will in all likelihood not relate to your own actual ancestors at all. So, before you get carried away and think you have found ancient and noble connections, with a coat of arms and an ancestral 'palace' to boot, be extremely cautious.

A redeeming feature is that the Indexes to the Harleian Manuscripts can be searched from this site. These documents were collected by Edward and Robert Harley, the first two Earls of Oxford, between the mid-17th and mid-18th centuries, and are now lodged in the British Museum.

This site is included here more as a warning than a recommendation, although it is unfair to single out this particular website. The author wishes to make it clear that it is included as being representative of a genre, which may be considered entertaining but is unlikely to be based on serious individual genealogical research.

www.genserv.com
GenServ Genealogical GEDCOM Server System

Overall rating: ★ ★			
Classification:	Name-search	Readability:	★ ★
Updating:	Occasionally	Content:	★ ★
Navigation:	★ ★	Speed:	★ ★ ★

US

This very cluttered, very confusing, very colourful site is daunting, to say the least, though a little persistence may be rewarded. If you like your sites busily spattered with exclamation marks, this may be for you. Others will find it a perfect example of how not to create a website. A free trial membership is possible for an introductory period, after which a modest subscription is charged. The site is run by Cliff Manis from Texas, whose frilly white beard matches that of the little Santa Claus figure seen in his photograph. In Suffolk, however, he has a colleague named Jon Rees who handles European membership and postal queries. What Cliff has created is a database of individual GEDCOM files, to which you can add your own and through which you can consult others. Communications from GenServ are made to you via email.

SPECIAL FEATURES

How to Join outlines four steps, the first of which is 'Create a GEDCOM file', and then gives three further stages for submitting it. Full access is denied until a GEDCOM file has been submitted. If creating a GEDCOM file is a new task, select Documentation from the yellow tabs near the top of the homepage and then scroll down to GEDMAKE, last in the list on that page. This is useful and, to judge from the sample pages shown, the presentation calms down considerably once you are into the system.

Customer Support introduces the volunteers who work alongside Cliff to keep the site up to date, one of them being Jon Rees. Alongside his photo there are several links, including those to his own webpage and family tree page.

Visitor Information, about four lines down from the top of the homepage, is probably the best place to start.

Very American, very repetitive, this site keeps going round in circles and is not immediately easy to use, but there are good things in here and you may just happen upon another user who is researching the same family tree. Worth a try.

OTHER SITES OF INTEREST

Obituary Archive Search Engine
www.obitcentral.com/obitsearch

The Obituary Daily Times
www.rootsweb.com/~obituary

The two US-based websites above are, so far, the only obituary searches going back more than just a few years. They may be of some use, however, if you have ancestors who emigrated.

International Internet Genealogical Society
www.iigs.org/index.htm.en
This website, which was still under construction at the time of writing, promises to be most useful. A mission statement and the early beginnings of the site can already be viewed at www.iigs.org. The IIGS is a voluntary organisation planning to create a multilingual facility to share genealogical research on the internet and promote worldwide cooperation.

SEE ALSO

The Journal of Online Genealogy (see p. 135)
www.onlinegenealogy.com

Family Tree Maker (see p. 38)
www.familytreemaker.com or
www.bannerblue.com

Genealogy.com (see p. 39)
www.genealogy.com

Family Search (see p. 32)
www.familysearch.org

Useful addresses

The Guild of One-Name Studies
Box G
14 Charterhouse Building
Goswell Road
London
EC1M 7BA
email: *guild@one-name.org*

Chapter 5

war and the services

The first port of call for anyone researching an ancestor who served in the British Army, Navy, Royal Marines or Merchant Navy must be the Public Record Office at Kew (see p. 35).

Army Lists have been published almost annually since 1754, though, unfortunately, many records were lost in a bombing raid during the Second World War. The earliest Navy Records date back to the mid-seventeeth century. Both groups of records are held at the PRO.

Records from the two World Wars are held at the Family Records Centre (see p. 31) and current, or very recent, service records are held at the Ministry of Defence (see p. 90). Recent and current records, however, are not normally available to the general public.

In addition to these national holdings, there are several other good collections. The websites that follow are all of a noticeably high standard and will thoroughly reward exploration. It is important when searching for a particular ancestor, rather than merely seeking information about the wider historical picture, that you are as accurate as possible about the name, dates of service and regiment or ship(s) with which your ancestor was associated.

www.cwgc.org
Commonwealth War Graves Commission

Overall rating: ★ ★ ★ ★			
Classification:	Name-search	**Readability:**	★ ★ ★ ★ ★
Updating:	Regularly	**Content:**	★ ★ ★ ★ ★
Navigation:	★ ★ ★	**Speed:**	★ ★ ★ ★

UK

Looking sombre against a grey background, this website's homepage, with its small print, may appear difficult to read. However, don't be put off; subsequent pages are easier and extremely informative. The various items in the Contents column down the left of the page include The Task, Horticulture, Architecture, Global Commitment and a profile of Sir Fabian Ware, who was responsible for the idea of the Commission. Scrolling right down this column, to below the wreaths of poppies, brings up the last option, the Debt of Honour Register, which is probably where you want to be.

SPECIAL FEATURES

Debt of Honour Register has an explanatory front page and a Search the Register link in purple at the foot of it. In the search boxes that this produces, a search will be triggered almost regardless of how limited the information you give, particularly if the surname you are searching for is not too common. Note, though, that using an initial in the second box may cause problems unless you are absolutely certain of it, because the computer selects only those names for whom the given initial comes first. If the person you are seeking was commonly known by a second name and you enter that initial, you will not find the right connection.

Each time a record is found, it gives details of rank, number, force, date of death and age. It also gives details of parents (if known) and approximate address (town and county), spouse if married, and may give a little more by way of education or profession. Finally, it gives details of the cemetery where the casualty is buried and basic directions for finding it.

At this point, it may be worth going back to Services and Links in the Contents column to see what further information may be available from the Commission, now that you have better details of the casualty you are seeking. For instance, the exact location of individual graves is normally available, and you may wish to click on the link to The Royal British Legion, for example, which helps arrange visits to war graves. Other links on the same page include The Imperial War Museum, The German War Graves Commission, Australian War Memorial and the Department of Internal Affairs, New Zealand.

Veterans Affairs, Canada and **Veterans Affairs, England** come right at the bottom of the page, and clicking on the latter takes you to the website of the Ministry of Defence. The quickest route to the information you want is then to click on 'search' in the tabs along the top of the homepage and type 'veterans' in the subsequent search box.

For anyone seeking details of a wartime casualty from any date from the First World War onwards, this is an invaluable resource, clearly and helpfully presented.

www.kcl.ac.uk/lhcma/top.htm.
King's College London Liddell Hart Centre for Military Archives

Overall rating: ★★★★★			
Classification:	Records	**Readability:**	★★★★
Updating:	Regularly	**Content:**	★★★★★
Navigation:	★★★★	**Speed:**	★★★★★

(UK)

Based around the library collections of Captain Sir Basil Liddell Hart, the Centre now holds the archives of around 500 distinguished 20th-century British defence personnel.

SPECIAL FEATURES

For internal research purposes, you are invited to give your name and the reason for visiting the site, but this is entirely voluntary. If you don't want to do so, simply put an 'X' in the name box and press 'submit'. Next click on 'Continue to Home Page'.

What Can You Find Here? gives a brief overview of the collections.

List of the Collections, a little further down the page, is more informative, starting with a long list of the papers pertaining to each individual, listed alphabetically by name. The contents of some, but not all, of these can be consulted in more detail by clicking on the words 'detailed catalogue' in blue alongside the relevant entries. Following this is a list of other documents, catalogued by title, of which basic details are available online.

What do I have to do to Consult Original Material? explains the necessarily slightly restricted access that is available, and which requires a letter of recommendation from a suitable referee. No actual records can be consulted online, so a visit in person is necessary.

Excellent, sometimes remarkable, material is available here for the family historian seeking to build up a picture of war during the 20th century.

www.regiments.org/milhist/index.htm

Regiments.org - Land Forces of Britain, the Empire and Commonwealth

Overall rating: ★ ★ ★ ★ ★

Classification:	History	Readability:	★ ★ ★ ★ ★
Updating:	Regularly	Content:	★ ★ ★
Navigation:	★ ★ ★	Speed:	★ ★ ★ ★

UK

This website explains in detail the British regimental system throughout the world, past and present. For genealogists it has probably two uses; first, it gives general information about the structure and practice of the army within a military history context, and, second, it helps you track down recent ancestors who may have served in the army.

SPECIAL FEATURES

Site Map (as the homepage is titled whenever you want to return to it) explains that there are several thousand links from this website 'bringing together all internet resources

pertaining to land forces that were at any time part of the British Empire or Commonwealth'. Naval and air forces are not included in the site, except where they have land- force elements.

Questions, in the top-of-page tabs, is the link to FAQs, of which the third is, How can I find out more about an ancestor who served in the British Army? Clicking on that question leads to a huge index of links, towards the bottom of which is a section headed Research Collections and Guides. Here several sources of help are listed, including the Ministry of Defence (see p. 90), the Public Record Office (see p. 35) and, further down the list, independent researchers who specialise in military records.

This website is outstanding for its huge number of relevant links, and it is a vital resource for anyone researching an ancestor who served in the army.

www.lightinfantry.org
British Light Infantry Regiments

Overall rating: ★ ★ ★ ★			
Classification:	Regiments	**Readability:**	★ ★ ★ ★ ★
Updating:	Regularly	**Content:**	★ ★ ★ ★
Navigation:	★ ★ ★ ★	**Speed:**	★ ★ ★ ★

UK

Mike Young runs this practical, efficient site, which turns out to be much more extensive than it at first appears.

SPECIAL FEATURES

Table of Contents This comes last in the red list on the homepage, and clicking here will give you an idea of the scope of the site. The early items refer to Mike Young's own family research, but thereafter there is a long list of links associated with each successive Light Infantry Regiment, often with onward links as well.

The 6th Battalion The (Somerset and Cornwall) Light Infantry (Volunteers), The 43rd Wessex (WW2) Association and **The Durham Light Infantry Association** These three special sections are below the picture on the homepage.

For background history or other material relating to any of the Light Infantry Regiments, this excellent website deserves exploration.

www.ships.co.uk/index.html

Ships.co.uk - Royal Navy Historical Pages

Overall rating: ★ ★ ★ ★

Classification:	Ships	**Readability:**	★ ★ ★ ★
Updating:	Occasionally	**Content:**	★ ★ ★ ★
Navigation:	★ ★ ★	**Speed:**	★ ★ ★ ★

UK

Subtitled 'Information for the Naval Enthusiast and Researcher', this website is useful for finding out about specific ships, as well as a certain amount about the people who served on them.

SPECIAL FEATURES

The two white boxes near the top of the homepage offer access to Shipping Today and Yesterday, the magazine for naval enthusiasts, and to Shipwatch Directory, a directory listing 39,000 current ships.

Below this are the Royal Navy Historical Pages, including English Ships at the Battle of Trafalgar 1805 and Ships in the News 150 Years Ago.

Royal Navy Ship Associations is where you can find out about reunions, while Ship Losses lists those ships to have gone down, divided and listed by date. It would be helpful to be able to search by individual ship name.

More a website for the family historian than the genealogist, this is certainly the right place to come for an overview of British naval history.

www.angelfire.com/de/BobSanders/MARIND.html

Bob Sanders' Family History Web Maritime Index

Overall rating: ★ ★ ★

Classification:	History	**Readability:**	★ ★ ★ ★
Updating:	Occasionally	**Content:**	★ ★ ★
Navigation:	★ ★ ★ ★	**Speed:**	★ ★ ★ ★

UK

This site has a Welsh, in particular Cardiff, emphasis, but would still be of use to anyone starting to look for information about mariners, Customs and Excise Officers, Coastguards and the like.

SPECIAL FEATURES

Each homepage link, under headings such as Tracing Records of 19th Century Merchant Mariners, Tracing the Deaths of Merchant Seamen at Sea and Tracing Records of Royal Navy Ratings, goes to a brief article explaining what the relevant records contain and where they may be consulted. The records themselves are not available for reading online. In some cases relevant website addresses to explore are given, though, again, direct online links are not available. This limitation explains its overall three-star status.

Although limited in its function, this is still a good directory of resources for anyone seeking information about sailors or others connected with the maritime world.

www.iwm.org.uk
Imperial War Museum

Overall rating: ★ ★ ★			
Classification: Records		**Readability:**	★ ★ ★ ★
Updating: Occasionally		**Content:**	★ ★ ★
Navigation: ★ ★		**Speed:**	★ ★ ★

UK

No time is wasted here with elaborate introductions. The homepage is brief and, apart from logos (which do offer links) to the half-dozen individual museums, including the Cabinet War Rooms and HMS Belfast, the only thing on offer is a Search All Sites button.

SPECIAL FEATURES

Search All Sites Clicking here brings up a page headed 'Search the Imperial War Museum website' on which there is a single search box. The search engine is rapid enough, though perhaps not all that sophisticated: entering 'Royal Engineers in India', for instance, brought up 323 matches, including all the appearances of the word 'in'! Observing the only search tip given, which is to put quotation marks round phrases, produced no matches at all. Going back to the original search but taking out the word 'in' reduced the number of matches to 75, but still each appearance of the word 'Royal' was listed, so that in the end the solution was to enter only 'India', producing a manageable seven results.

Imperial War Museum - Family History Research offers a link to Printed Books, of which the museum apparently holds more than 100,000. Here, there is only a brief description of what the collection contains, and it is limited to 20th-century conflict.

Even if you think a visit in person to the Imperial War Museum might be of use, this website will not do very much to decide you one way or the other. The search facility has its limitations but persistence could produce a useful result.

www.mod.uk/forces/records/army.htm		
Ministry of Defence		
Overall rating: ★ ★ ★		
Classification: Records	**Readability:**	★ ★ ★
Updating: Regularly	**Content:**	★ ★ ★ ★
Navigation: ★ ★ ★	**Speed:**	★ ★ ★
(UK)		

Subtitled 'How to Obtain British Army Service Records, Medals and Information', this is itself only a limited resource for anyone tracking an ancestor who served in UK forces at home or overseas. Nearly all past records, except the very recent, whose access is an any case restricted, are lodged with the Public Record Office (see p. 35).

SPECIAL FEATURES

Clicking on the individual services below the subtitle, however, brings up lists of places to contact besides the PRO, with links, for instance, to the Imperial War Museum, the Fleet Air Arm Museum, and so on.

Archive, in the purple header box, is not as helpful to the genealogist as Search. Here, typing Durham Light Infantry, for example, produced a link to the regimental museum website at the top of the list and several other links of variable relevance. Incidentally, pressing return on your keyboard will not activate a search; you must click on the 'Find' button. Links leads to a long list of Armed Forces worldwide, but all contemporary rather than historical.

There is relatively little to be gleaned here for the genealogist – hence the modest overall star-rating – since the emphasis of the website is to inform about present-day forces rather than those of the past, but it may be a route to some useful further links.

www.remembering.org/index.html		
The Remembering Project		
Overall rating: ★		
Classification: Records	**Readability:**	★
Updating: n/a	**Content:**	★
Navigation: ★	**Speed:**	★
(UK)		

The object of this website, founded by David Colwell, is to compile memories of the Second World War and the people who served in it. When the site was tested most of the links were not working, and a yellow note indicated that they were in the process of being replaced. This explains the minimal star-ratings above.

The site should not be confused with www.remember.org, which is listed opposite.

SPECIAL FEATURES

Access to Four Bulletin Boards suggests that the project is being greatly expanded. Dave Clark is in charge, and both he and David Colwell can be contacted by email. When Remembering Project Chat, Remembering Battle of Britain, Searching the RP, Historical Reference Library and Links and Bibliographies are working, this would no doubt be a useful website.

Come here, once the site is up to speed again, to seek recollections of relatives who fought in the Second World War, and to read up on the history and conduct of that war.

OTHER SITES OF INTEREST

Military History Research Institute
www.geocities.com/RainForest/Vines/2750/milhis.htm

This website is maintained by Chris Formaggia and lists various military units and individual personnel currently being researched either by him or others. In each case an email contact is given.

Stuart Tamblin
http://ourworld.compuserve.com/homepages/Stuart_Tamblin

Stuart Tamblin is a family historian specialising in military and 19th-century criminal research. He obligingly lists all the books, microfiches and databases in his possession, any single one of which he will search free of charge on your behalf.

Friends of War Memorials
www.war-memorials.com

Founded by Ian Davidson, FOM is dedicated to the preservation of war memorials. There is no name-search facility here, but the good list of Links (last item in the left-hand margin) makes the site worth visiting.

Cybrary of the Holocaust
www.remember.org

This site exists to commemorate victims of the Holocaust. It has recently introduced a Search and Unite link, which may be a route to finding out more about a survivor of the camps, or discovering a descendant of a survivor or victim.

Chapter 6

other special interest sources

This chapter contains a small number of websites that don't seem to belong elsewhere in the book but which could still be important. Several relate to royalty or the nobility. If it seems unlikely that these will be of any interest, remember that every family tree, if it can be traced back widely enough and far enough, will link with a royal line eventually.

Dr Brian Sykes, an Oxford University academic, who specialises in the study of genetics, has propounded the latest theory about how we are all interrelated. Using mitochondrial DNA samples, he has discovered that people sharing the same surnames are actually far more closely related than has ever previously been suspected. An early finding was that the 9,000-year-old skeleton known as Cheddar Man was closely related, in DNA terms, to a schoolteacher living less than a mile away from where the skeleton was found. This prompted Dr Sykes to write to 250 men in Yorkshire, Cheshire and Lancashire who shared his surname, sending them tiny brushes and asking them to return samples of a few cells scraped from inside the mouth. To his amazement he found that the 61 returns all shared the same genetic fingerprint.

This study has now been hugely extended and Dr Sykes believes, on the strength of some 6,000 samples, that all the peoples of Europe are descended from seven women. This incredible discovery is of huge potential importance to genealogists, as it opens up completely new ancestor-tracing possibilities. The relevant article about this discovery, from The Times of 19 April 2000, can be read, incidentally, on the Deja News website (see p. 142).

www.worldroots.com

WorldRoots Genealogy Archive

Overall rating: ★ ★ ★ ★

Classification:	Royalty	Readability:	★★★★
Updating:	Regularly	Content:	★★★★
Navigation:	★★★★	Speed:	★★★★

US

Created by Brigitte Gastel Lloyd out of a fascination for her own royal and other notable connections, this is a huge database of information about the Royal Dynasties of Europe and even some further afield, as will be seen from the list on the Site Map and General Index page.

At the bottom of the homepage is a search box that gives access to an apparently very sophisticated search facility. A test using the name of a fairly obscure personal ancestor linking to a royal line in the 18th century caused no problems at all – the right results came up immediately.

SPECIAL FEATURES

Brigitte Gastel Lloyd's Genealogy Pages Clicking here lets you find out more about Brigitte, but if she makes herself out to be somewhat fey and romantic here, the rest of her website is entirely practical, disciplined and serious.

Links includes European Royalty and Nobility from A to Z, Direct Access to Royal and Nobility Databases and What's New in Royal Genealogy, which has access to recently added royal photographs (not all recently taken) and paintings. Other links go to German Resources, Argentina Information and South America.

A very worthwhile specialist site for any research into royal connections.

www.baronage.co.uk
The Baronage Press

Overall rating: ★ ★ ★			
Classification:	Nobility	**Readability:**	★ ★ ★ ★
Updating:	Occasionally	**Content:**	★ ★ ★ ★
Navigation:	★ ★ ★	**Speed:**	★ ★ ★

UK

The Baronage Press has stepped in to do what Burke's Peerage no longer does, since its adoption by Halbert's, namely to offer information to help people establish connections with noble lines or, more often, disabuse them of the notion that they might have such connections.

SPECIAL FEATURES

The Press produces an online magazine called The Baronage and a newsletter called The Feudal Herald. The links to these are some way down the homepage under Magazine and Newsletter. Click on the words rather than on the logos above them.

Further still down the homepage is a link to Part 2 of the Home Page, in purple letters. This leads to an article exposing the dangers of being taken in by 'scams', such as the peddling of false coats of arms, lordships and other noble titles.

Returning to the central links below the logos, now click on Mists of Antiquity, and then on the third chapter, Debrett's and Burke's, which tells the sad story of the demise of these once great names.

Though not a research service as such, this gives good warnings about the pitfalls you may encounter in trying to establish noble connections.

www.royal.gov.uk
The British Monarchy

Overall rating: ★ ★ ★			
Classification:	Royalty	**Readability:**	★ ★ ★ ★
Updating:	Occasionally	**Content:**	★ ★ ★ ★
Navigation:	★ ★ ★	**Speed:**	★ ★ ★

UK

This, the official website of the British Monarchy, is likely to be of little use to researchers except for tracing their descent once they have 'collided' with a royal line, but then all family trees, if traced laterally and sufficiently far back in time, do in fact do that sooner or later. For these purposes see Monarchy Through the Ages in the red index boxes. The first of the red index boxes to appear is that for the late Diana Princess of Wales, but probably more relevant for researchers should be the last box, Search, which is still apparently being 'refined'. This, however, is only going to transport the user back to www.open.gov.uk (see p. 41), and is not one of the most helpful links.

This is a site of limited interest where far more could be done to help the genealogical researcher. However, it may offer some entertaining moments as you trawl around, such as giving the answers to questions like, 'Why does the Queen keep corgis?'

www.genealogy.ukgateway.net
David Pacey's Genealogy Website

Overall rating: ★ ★ ★			
Classification:	Executions	**Readability:**	★ ★
Updating:	Occasionally	**Content:**	★ ★ ★ ★
Navigation:	★ ★	**Speed:**	★ ★ ★ ★

UK

David Pacey's website is concerned with tracing his own family tree, mainly in Lincolnshire, but it also has a section on Executions in UK and Ireland. You need an Adobe Acrobat Reader (see p. 22) to access this information, and you also need to email David to obtain a password in order to open the files. The low star-score above reflects the limited nature of the information available to the general user and the complications of access, and not any inadequacy of the site as a whole.

Useful for the online information about executions.

www.english-heritage.org.uk
English Heritage

Overall rating: ★ ★ ★			
Classification:	Monuments	**Readability:**	★ ★ ★ ★ ★
Updating:	Regularly	**Content:**	★ ★ ★ ★ ★
Navigation:	★ ★ ★ ★ ★	**Speed:**	★ ★ ★ ★ ★

UK

From the point of view of the genealogical researcher, the most useful part of this website is undoubtedly the National Monuments Record, listed as the last link on the homepage. The Royal Commission on the Historical Monuments of England (RCHM) is creating this public archive of all the monuments under its care; it already holds 12 million items.

SPECIAL FEATURES

The National Monuments Record Thesauri and MIDAS (Monument Inventory Data Standard) pages, accessed from the National Monuments Record link, explain in academic detail the policy employed for the recording of this material. This would, of course, be of considerable relevance to a local history society, for instance, whose members proposed to record the monuments in their parish churchyard.

For the private individual the usefulness of English Heritage probably lies in the National Monuments Record public search rooms in London or Swindon, whose holdings can be found online, but the texts of which are not available without visiting in person, or consulting their publications. What's New lists the most recent of these and forthcoming events.

Perhaps of limited use for genealogical purposes, which is the only thing downgrading its overall star-rating, this is still an excellently clear and inspiring website, around which navigation is rewardingly rapid.

www.dcs.hull.ac.uk/public/genealogy

Royal and Noble Genealogical Data on the Web

Overall rating: ★ ★ ★			
Classification: Royalty		**Readability:**	★★★★
Updating: Occasionally		**Content:**	★★★★
Navigation: ★★★		**Speed:**	★★★

UK

Brian Tompsett in the Department of Computer Science at Hull University maintains this website, which lists all the sources of genealogical data about Royal Families (British and other).

SPECIAL FEATURES

A quick run through the extensive index on the homepage will give an immediate idea of the vast amount of material available. Links load relatively slowly, but some are well worth waiting for. They are usefully divided into those sites that are, and are not, of genealogical relevance.

Royal Descents of famous people leads to the chatty, though interesting, thoughts of Mark Humphrys, who explains that because all humanity is interrelated many times over and that 'what is documented continuously is of course only the royalty and nobility', everyone will find a link to a royal line eventually. At the end of the Introduction is a section headed Ancestors and Descendants, after which there is a further link to What Is The Point Of Genealogy? This, for anyone not already converted, is well worth reading.

If you are exploring the ancestry of royal houses, whether in the UK or elsewhere, this will prove to be most useful.

OTHER SITES OF INTEREST

The Royal Commission on the Ancient and Historical Monuments of Scotland
www.rcahms.gov.uk/about.html

English Heritage National Monuments Record
www.imagesofengland.org.uk
This is a Year 2000 future project to build a photographic record of 360,000 listed buildings. Volunteer photographers, who are all members of the Royal Photographic Society, are taking part. The website is as yet only partially constructed.

Chapter 7

research services

Most of the websites in this chapter do not restrict themselves to the provision of research services, though they do all have such a function as a major part of their operations. Most of them also offer numerous links to further genealogical information, while some sell publications or software. In fact, you could argue that virtually every website in this book offers research services, in the sense of making information freely available, but the sites featured here provide specific, one-to-one assistance.

This assistance is offered in two ways. There are many individuals and a few organisations who will carry out genealogical research on your behalf. Usually you have to pay for this help, though quite often an assessment of the likelihood of any success will be given first, with an estimate of cost. In these cases, you do not have to commit yourself to paying until you decide whether it will be worthwhile. You can often arrange to pay in instalments as you see the progress of the research effort, or agree to pay in the first instance up to an agreed limit and only authorise further payments later. Factors that will influence your decision will be related either to the difficulty of finding out the information for yourself, or to the cost in time and possibly in travel and accommodation costs that would be incurred if you carried out the same research yourself. Against this background the fees often seem very moderate.

The importance of assuring yourself of the professional credentials of anyone you employ to do this sort of work cannot be over-stressed. There are many highly skilled, highly professional researchers out there ready to help you. There are also untrained amateurs trying to jump on what they see as a gravy-train.

The other sort of service that is available here is record-collecting and transmitting, usually by post but sometimes by email, in cases where you have already identified the documents you want and simply need someone else to pick them up and send them on to you. Some of these services make regular courier runs to the most-used record holdings, such as those at the Family Records Centre. Costs depend to a great extent on the speed with which you want the copied documents to reach you. If you are not in a hurry, fees can be extremely reasonable.

www.college-of-arms.gov.uk
College of Arms

Overall rating: ★ ★ ★ ★			
Classification:	Heraldry	Readability:	★★★★★
Updating:	Regularly	Content:	★★★★★
Navigation:	★★★★★	Speed:	★★★★★

UK

The rather faded colours come as a surprise and perhaps a relief after the glaring tones of so many websites, but the information is highly professional and clear, as you would expect from so august a body.

SPECIAL FEATURES

Frequently Asked Questions (on the homepage top tabs or again at the bottom of the page) number only three: Do coats of arms belong to surnames? What are the pantone numbers for the colours used in heraldry? What is a crest?

About the College of Arms is the most informative part of the site, within which are found links to The Granting of Arms (number eight in the list) and Having a Coat of Arms or Crest Identified (number eleven).

Enquiries offers an email facility for asking questions.

Links include British Library Manuscript Collections, The British Monarchy - The Official Website, House of Lords Record Office and Royal Commission on Historical Manuscripts among others.

If you wish to establish a right to a coat of arms, or to identify a coat of arms borne by an ancestor, this is unquestionably the place to come.

www.ihgs.ac.uk

The Institute of Heraldic and Genealogical Studies

Overall rating: ★ ★ ★ ★			
Classification:	Heraldry	**Readability:**	★ ★ ★ ★ ★
Updating:	Occasionally	**Content:**	★ ★ ★ ★ ★
Navigation:	★ ★ ★ ★	**Speed:**	★ ★ ★ ★ ★

UK

Founded in 1961 by the irrepressible and splendidly-named Cecil Humphery-Smith, the Institute runs courses and tutorial days as well as maintaining a most useful Library (30,000 items, many unique).

SPECIAL FEATURES

Courses includes an extremely thorough correspondence course (with a few tutorial days) leading to the Institute's Diploma in Genealogy and, at a higher level, Licenciateship of the Institute.

Genetic Research explains the Institute's extremely valuable work investigating the hereditary aspects of such conditions as blastoglaucoma, schizophrenia and Alzheimer's disease, as well as some cancers.

Publications includes Humphery-Smith's own works on the bearing of arms, past and present – one is rather charmingly reviewed as 'a book that all dedicated amorists (sic) should make room for...' – and the indispensable Phillimore Atlas and Index of Parish Registers. The Institute also publishes its own annual Family History Diary, numerous useful maps and several teacher's packs, as well as a 'genealogical simulation exercise' called 'The Elephant Hunt', which takes students through the process of tracing a fictional family named Elephant, step-by-step.

Under Heraldic Research, which is a particular strength of the Institute, are also Palaeography (the interpretation of early documents) and Handwriting Analysis; the Institute can help with both.

This fine organisation, which, in web terms, might be called old-style British, was founded as the result of one man's passion for genealogy, and it adheres to his standards of excellence and reliability.

www.achievements.co.uk
Achievements of Canterbury

Overall rating: ★ ★ ★ ★			
Classification:	Heraldry	Readability:	★ ★ ★ ★
Updating:	Occasionally	Content:	★ ★ ★ ★
Navigation:	★ ★ ★ ★	Speed:	★ ★ ★ ★

UK

Based in Canterbury, Achievements was established some 40 years ago, making it the oldest genealogical research organisation of its kind. It is linked with the Institute of Heraldic and Genealogical Studies (see p. 101), whose work it supports, and all its researchers are fully IHGS trained. For a fee, Achievements will help you with anything from sorting out a sticky patch in your research to creating an entire pedigree.

SPECIAL FEATURES

Welcome is partly devoted to publicising the various television and radio programmes of interest to genealogy enthusiasts, a useful shortcut to finding out what is currently being broadcast.

Services not only includes tracing ancestors, but also such tasks as establishing the right to bear a Coat of Arms, tracing missing heirs or relatives, transcribing or translating old handwriting, researching the history of your house or locality, and even advising on the purchase of lordships and baronies. Achievements can provide a fully 'scrivened' family tree (that is, which includes calligraphic script, handmade paper, heraldic artwork) or create for you an individual Family History book.

Visit Us gives details of the Heraldry Centre in Northgate, Canterbury, where you can arrange a 'consultation' if your research has run aground. Here they will also organise special tours, principally for visitors from abroad, going to the villages, churches and possibly even the homes where ancestors lived.

Links will connect to Search and Unite, run by David Lewin in London and Margret Chatwin in Munich, whose aim is to find and reunite people who became separated during the Second World War (work is charged at £10 per hour). This website itself links to www.remember.org (see p. 91), whose objective is to commemorate Holocaust victims and keep survivors in touch with each other.

The Royal Commission on Historical Manuscripts link leads to the National Register of Archives, part of the Historical Manuscripts Commission (see p. 116).

The long-established and professionally staffed nature of this research organisation makes it a reliable choice for those needing some support in taking their research forward.

www.agra.org.uk
The Association of Genealogists and Record Agents

Overall rating: ★ ★ ★ ★			
Classification: Research		**Readability:**	★ ★ ★ ★
Updating: Regularly		**Content:**	★ ★ ★ ★
Navigation: ★ ★ ★ ★		**Speed:**	★ ★ ★ ★

`UK`

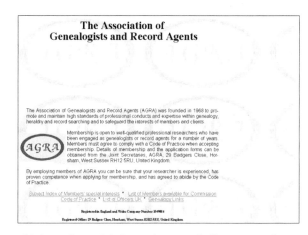

This is a safe, straightforward route to finding a researcher to help you with your search in whatever field interests you. Total confidentiality is assured.

Founded in 1968 to promote expertise in the fields of genealogy, heraldry and record searching, AGRA lists only those researchers who meet specified standards of competence and comply with AGRA's own Code of Practice (see link on the homepage). By employing any AGRA member to help you in your research, therefore, you are guaranteed a certain level of professionalism. The price you pay is agreed with the researcher, who will either estimate for a defined task or will agree an expenditure limit where the task is more open-ended. Only the relatively limited remit of the site accounts for the overall four-star rather than five-star rating.

SPECIAL FEATURES

Subject Index of Members' special interests links to a list of specialisms that include everything from Anglo-Indians to Gypsy History, Intestacy to Missionary Records, and the Pottery Industry to University Alumni. Each of these has a code or codes alongside it, and these identify the researchers who specialise in that particular field. Make a note of the relevant codes, therefore, go to the bottom of the page and click on List of Members Available for Commission, and then scroll down to the correct entries. The codes are given alphabetically and then numerically after each name.

www.gendocs.demon.co.uk

GenDocs Genealogical Research in England and Wales

Overall rating: ★ ★ ★ ★			
Classification:	Research	**Readability:**	★ ★ ★ ★
Updating:	Regularly	**Content:**	★ ★ ★ ★
Navigation:	★ ★ ★ ★	**Speed:**	★ ★ ★ ★

UK

John and Elaine Hitchcock, who run this very useful service from their home in Northampton, founded GenDocs in 1992 and have had a website since 1994. They supply genealogical documents worldwide both to private individuals and to research agencies or family history societies. They specialise in English and Welsh ancestry and run a daily courier service in London to all the major archive holdings. They also supply photographs of buildings and monuments in London and the South Midlands. An area of particular personal interest and expertise is Victorian London. Contact is currently by post, not email.

SPECIAL FEATURES

Courier Service, in the left-of-page index, explains that GenDocs will collect copies of documents from The Family Records Centre, London Metropolitan Archives, The Principal Registry of the Family Division, the Guildhall Library and the City of Westminster Archives Centre, though not from the Public Record Office at Kew. Details of charges are available under Courier Prices.

BMD Certificates, Census Returns, Wills & Admons and **Parish Registers** These few items in the index have good, brief explanatory notes: Research Service explains in more detail what GenDocs can do for you, and Research Aids leads to the Hitchcocks' particular field, Victorian London.

Glossaries These are two very useful features located in the right-of-page yellow boxes. One explains abbreviations and acronyms commonly found in genealogy, the other the meanings of the names of ranks, trades and professions.

Census Returns for England and Wales 1841-1901 lays out the exact sequence of questions asked in each Census, a good guide to what information you can expect if you order a Census return for an ancestor at whatever Census date.

Wayne Fulton's Scanning Tips, at the bottom of the yellow list, links to a very clear and helpful explanation of how to get the best from your scanner.

This could be an extremely useful service for those not able to get to London to pursue research but who have identified the documents they want.

www.geocities.com/Heartland/Plains/8555
The Parsonage Pages

Overall rating: ★ ★ ★ ★			
Classification:	Research	**Readability:**	★ ★ ★ ★ ★
Updating:	Regularly	**Content:**	★ ★ ★ ★
Navigation:	★ ★ ★ ★	**Speed:**	★ ★ ★ ★

(UK)

Based in Cheshire and with a wide knowledge of the Midlands, Helen Parsonage offers a lot of articulate and useful information, much of it of relevant to researchers nationwide.

SPECIAL FEATURES

Helen's Genealogy Pages links to a very good list of Midlands resources, followed by some general links to those websites she finds she consults most frequently. The remainder of the homepage index relates mainly to her own specific family tree interests, with particular emphasis on Cheshire.

The Look-Up Exchange For general use, however, this is an extraordinarily useful facility, in which volunteers nationwide offer to consult the records at their disposal, free of charge. This means either that they own good collections of reference works themselves or that they will visit local libraries, record offices or other organisations within their area on your behalf. Click first on the country in which you are seeking information: England, Wales, Scotland or the Isle of Man, then on the relevant county. This produces an alphabetical list of towns, with details of the records and names of the researchers available to help you. Once you have located a record you wish to consult, clicking on the name, in blue letters, of the relevant volunteer researcher will lead to an email message facility.

The Parsonage Book Pages, at the bottom of the homepage index, is also worth consulting. As indicated, it is a link to Amazon.co.uk, but in addition to the general search facility there are several books listed that Helen has selected as particularly useful, with her own notes saying why.

When it seems hard to justify a journey to some distant corner of the country to consult what may be only a single record, click here and look for a volunteer based in that area to help you. A wonderful idea, professionally managed.

www.backtoroots.co.uk

Back to Roots Family History Service

Overall rating: ★ ★ ★			
Classification: Research		**Readability:**	★ ★ ★
Updating: Occasionally		**Content:**	★ ★ ★
Navigation: ★ ★ ★		**Speed:**	★ ★ ★ ★

UK

Mike Portlock maintains this service, which supplies family history products (books, recording aids, computer software) and can also provide the services of professional researchers.

SPECIAL FEATURES

Running a weekly courier service to the Family Records Centre, Back to Roots will find such documents as Census returns and wills on your behalf. Search Services (small green lettering in the left-of-page index) indicates the cost, and offers a £6.50 refund if they fail to find a certificate.

Prices are lower the more accurately you can specify the range of years in which to search.

Software Sales is simply a list, without critical assessments, of software applications, but includes a useful index of material available on CDs and disks. Among these are several Pigot's Directories and Kelly's Trade Directories.

Books and Paper Sales links to an extensive list, though again without assessment, under six headings: Books, Criminal Register Indexes (providing a quick answer to 'those illusive (sic) ancestors!'), Militia Musters, Prisoners Pardoned, PRO Names and Others.

Enquiry Form Online ordering is available here.

A useful service for those who can't easily get to the Family Records Centre or those whose genealogical research has reached the stage of identifying specific documents to consult.

http://ourworld.compuserve.com/homepages /dave_tylcoat/handwrit.htm			
Early English Handwriting			
Overall rating: ★ ★ ★			
Classification:	Information	**Readability:**	★ ★ ★
Updating:	Occasionally	**Content:**	★ ★ ★
Navigation:	★ ★ ★	**Speed:**	★ ★ ★

UK

Maintained by Dave and Sue Tylcoat, this website illustrates the problem of reading early handwriting, using a number of examples taken from the 16th and 17th centuries. The information given here is interesting but limited, so the website earns its place more by virtue of the fact that it is one of very few on this topic.

SPECIAL FEATURES

Glossary leads to a short list of unfamiliar words regularly found in old documents. Some detail is given about how to tackle reading a difficult document, and where to get further information in the way of books to read. This, however, is not a 'translation' service.

The problem of reading old documents is a tricky one; there may also be further information found from the links in Cyndi's List (see p. 29): www.cyndislist.com/handwrit.htm

OTHER SITES OF INTEREST

Audrey Collins, BA
www.kenaud.dircon.co.uk
This genealogist has much knowledge of London and Middlesex. She is also interested in Australian connections.

Genfindit
www.genfindit.com
This is an online ordering service for copies of Scottish and Irish vital records. Not much about the service is available from the website but the testimonials from users read well.

Deciphering Old Handwriting
www.firstct.com/fv/oldhand.html
Try this site for more examples, some entertaining, of the difficulties in deciphering old handwriting. Sabina Murray is the tutor.

Some Tips on Reading Old Handwriting
www.sierra.com/sierrahome/familytree/hqarticles/handwriting
An article about deciphering old handwriting by Robert Davis in Heritage Quest magazine is available here for reading online.

www.brit-a-r.demon.co.uk
British Ancestral Research
Tim Cooper is a private researcher offering a one-price service and guaranteeing to trace two names in your family to at least four generations (or partial money back). The website gives straightforward information about the service, and contact details but no onward links.

SEE ALSO

UK Genealogy USA
www.ukgenealogyusa.free-online.co.uk
(p. 43)

Chapter 8
libraries

In a sense, nearly all the websites in this book are libraries. And they all contribute to make the internet what it is: a vast and, as yet, rather disorganised library of information, but one on which we are daily becoming more reliant. Some people fear that we shall, indeed, come to use the internet as our only library resource. They believe that, as a consequence, the wonderful riches in our actual libraries will simply disappear from our knowledge-bank because they have not been digitised for transmission on the web,

and that they will be known to only a few academics. Douglas Adams (yes, he of The Hitch-Hiker's Guide...) has said that the resultant loss of knowledge would be a catastrophe on the scale of the burning of The Great Library of Alexandria in ancient times. Let us hope he is wrong.

Libraries are, in any case, starting to fight back. Very, very few of the millions of books they collectively contain can be read online, but many libraries have been quick to put details of their catalogues on the web. This way, at least, they can tell us what they have that might illuminate our studies and enhance our researches.

www.eblast.com
Britannica.com

Overall rating: ★ ★ ★ ★ ★			
Classification:	Information	**Readability:**	★ ★ ★ ★
Updating:	Regularly	**Content:**	★ ★ ★ ★ ★
Navigation:	★ ★ ★ ★	**Speed:**	★ ★ ★ ★ ★

UK

This puts the massive resources of the Encyclopaedia Britannica literally at your fingertips.

SPECIAL FEATURES

There are two routes in: either simply fill in the search box at the top of the page and press Find, or select a category from the index list on the left of the page under Explore and follow the onward links. The information here is too extensive to list, but when everything else has failed this may be where to come! Incidentally, use '+' to link words when searching.

Refining your search accurately enough may be the problem here, with such a vast bank of data available, but it's worth a try.

www.bl.uk
The British Library

Overall rating: ★ ★ ★ ★ ★			
Classification: Libraries		**Readability:**	★ ★ ★ ★ ★
Updating: Regularly		**Content:**	★ ★ ★ ★ ★
Navigation: ★ ★ ★ ★		**Speed:**	★ ★ ★ ★

UK

Liberally adorned with photographs of the recently completed Library (physically almost next door to St Pancras Station in Marylebone, London), this attractive site's homepage starts with an Introducing the British Library option. Click on the down arrow to the right of the box and others in the list appear, including Visiting the Library in Person, What's Available Without a Visit and What's New. The pictures slow things down only slightly and do have the virtue of reminding the user of the Library's incomparable treasures. Navigation is inevitably somewhat complicated, due to the enormous complexity of the site, but the browser 'back' button works at great speed, so retracing one's steps is not difficult.

SPECIAL FEATURES

Search the Catalogues transports the user to OPAC 97 (Online Public Access Catalogue), part sponsored by Amazon.co.uk.

General Help Further down the first page, it is worth clicking on here before going further, as this offers a good first-stage explanation of how the 150 million items in the BL collections are divided.

Search the Collections By returning to the OPAC front page and clicking here, you will find a choice of nine collection categories, lodged either in London or in the Document Supply Collections at Boston Spa. If you know which category to search, clicking on the appropriate button will speed things up. Even if you don't, however, response times are exceptionally good. The form below, requesting author's name, title, subject, publisher and so on, need not be filled in completely to produce a result. Even filling a single box is enough on which to base a search, though refining it of course helps. Usefully, the number of search results is immediately posted, which gives you the chance to decide whether to track through them all or try refining.

Online, at the bottom of the homepage, brings up various options, including Inside, an exciting development that permits you to search the Library's entire journal and conference collection, order directly over the web, and receive articles within two hours. The database starts from 1973, holds 10 million documents and is expanding at the rate of 10,000 daily. Charges relate to the method of transmission, courier being the most expensive, first-class mail or 12-hour (as opposed to two-hour) fax the cheapest.

Gabriel is 'the gateway to Europe's national libraries', a resource of almost unimaginable scope.

Services, in the left-hand column index, brings up such delights as the Picture Library, where several hours of browsing could be happily spent (it offers transparencies for hire) while those who have the right audio equipment could enjoy the Sound Archive, found under Collections.

See also www.bl.uk/collections/newspaper for details of the large newspaper collections held at the British Library

This is a huge site, impossible to describe in full detail here, but one well worth visiting, especially if you have the name of a book or author you need to track down, or if there is a matter of historical background you wish to research.

www.earl.org.uk/familia			
Familia			
Overall rating: ★ ★ ★ ★			
Classification:	Libraries	**Readability:**	★ ★ ★ ★ ★
Updating:	Regularly	**Content:**	★ ★ ★ ★ ★
Navigation:	★ ★ ★ ★	**Speed:**	★ ★ ★ ★
UK			

The EARL Consortium uses its Family History Task Group to update and maintain this online directory of family history material held in British public libraries. Supporting partners with EARL include, for instance, the Public Record Office and the Library Association. On the date tested, the two Search Familia options were temporarily unavailable, but all the lists of source material are easily, clearly and immediately accessible.

SPECIAL FEATURES

The totally simple homepage offers only three locations on which to click: the logo, the sub-heading in bold print and the words Text Index. Go for Text Index unless you like flow-chart presentation, though the information from all three is the same.

Sources has excellent brief explanations of what will be found in, for instance, Census Returns, Parish Registers or Electoral Registers and Poll Books.

Links produces a useful list of connections to, for example, the Association of Genealogists and Record Agents at www.agra.org.uk (see p. 103) and the very useful MultiMap (see p. 144), which lets you pinpoint UK towns and villages, even if you do not know which county they are in, as well as London streets and GB postcode areas.

MuseumNet is, as yet, very limited in usefulness, because only a tiny number of the nation's museums are listed. John Fuller's Mailing List Website links to a list of genealogy resources on the internet of use to UK users, now hosted by RootsWeb.

This clear, simple, unflashy website has many uses, principally the directory of library contents but also some useful links.

www.tcwaters.free-online.co.uk/index.html
Ibertek

Overall rating: ★ ★ ★ ★			
Classification:	General	**Readability:**	★ ★ ★ ★ ★
Updating:	Regularly	**Content:**	★ ★ ★ ★
Navigation:	★ ★ ★ ★	**Speed:**	★ ★ ★ ★ ★

UK

This almost bafflingly large gateway website does everything any of the similar American sites do, with the great advantage that it is actually UK-based – in Whitby, North Yorkshire. It is maintained by T.C. Waters, publishers and distributors of computer, history and education products.

SPECIAL FEATURES

Enter Click this yellow button at the bottom of the home page to start exploring. The green buttons give access to a number of general categories, of which Genealogy Links 1

and 2 will be your best starting point. From the first of these a multitude of further links is given, carefully and logically sorted in a subject index that includes International Genealogy, Maritime Records, Maps & Topography and so on. Within each of these categories – for instance Isle of Man Genealogy listed under International Genealogy – another further list of links is given.

Here, you can find out about everything from deciphering Egyptian hieroglyphics to getting the letters of your own name put into as many anagrams as is humanly possible. Amazing!

Both fun and yet intensely serious, this site will seek out almost any genealogical resource you care to name. And if you are looking for something really obscure and no normal search engine has helped, see what T.C. Waters can do, because even if you don't find what you want, serendipity will lead you down some extraordinary avenues.

YOU HAVE REACHED THE

IBERTEK

WEBSITE

010729   LAST UPDATED 10 JUNE 2000

FAMILY HISTORY
LOCAL HISTORY
GENERAL HISTORY
IBERTEK GENEALOGY SOFTWARE
ON LINE VIRTUAL LIBRARY

www.odinscastle.org
Odin's Castle

Overall rating: ★ ★ ★ ★ ★			
Classification:	Historical	**Readability:**	★ ★ ★ ★
Updating:	Regularly	**Content:**	★ ★ ★ ★
Navigation:	★ ★ ★ ★	**Speed:**	★ ★ ★ ★

US

Although moving around a site that is a) so large and b) so decorative can be slow, the massive amount of historical information makes it more than worthwhile, as the huge list of awards in The Hall of Honor indicates.

Fully titled 'Odin's Castle of Dreams and Legends, an Archive of History and Historical Resources', and starting with the words, 'Heartfelt good morrow and welcome...' might suggest that this is not a serious site for the genealogist, or indeed for anyone. Certainly, with its 'ye olde worlde' illuminated manuscript appearance, it is eccentric. Paul Gwynn (Odin) starts by telling at great length the 'faery tale come true' that has just happened to him, falling in love with his Belgian wife Lieve, whom he met through the website. She is now creating pages of her own under, of course, the name Gwynnevere. You get the picture, and yet... scroll down the lengthy homepage and start looking at what the site contains.

SPECIAL FEATURES

The Dungeon, The Gatehouse, The Buttery and **The Privy**
Under these names, each of which fortunately has a subtitle giving a brief indication of the contents, is the most staggering amount of information, much of it leading to further links. As an example, visiting The Monk's Cell - The Crusades and the History of Religion (click on the door button) leads to nearly 20 references for the Crusades alone, moving on to such sites as that for the Knights Templar, the Online Reference Book for Medieval Studies and numerous others. Detailed description is impossible. It's simply up to you to explore.

http://ihr.sas.ac.uk/gh
Guildhall Library (Corporation of London) Manuscripts Section

Overall rating: ★ ★ ★ ★			
Classification:	Records	**Readability:**	★ ★ ★
Updating:	Regularly	**Content:**	★ ★ ★ ★
Navigation:	★ ★ ★	**Speed:**	★ ★ ★

UK

First click on General Guide to Collections, which explains (well down the page) the vital point to bear in mind, namely that the Manuscripts Section of the Guildhall Library is the local record office for the City of London (the geographical 'Square Mile') rather than the archives for the Corporation of London, which have their own Records Office (see below). The holdings date from the 11th century, and consist mainly of records associated with London's local and taxation authorities, livery companies, courts of law, churches, charities, schools and businesses. Note that the four-star rating above relates not to the content of the collections, which is undoubtedly five-star, but to the complications of finding one's way around the website.

SPECIAL FEATURES

Leaflet Guides to Records, also on the homepage, is another useful point from which to start. Each of the leaflets listed can be read in full online.

Other links go to Genealogical Sources at Guildhall Library, City of London Parish Records and Business Records at Guildhall Library, which date from the 15th century.

Livery Company Membership Guide goes to a page at the bottom of which is a further link to the actual list of companies, including, alongside the familiar trades, such obscure terms as 'loriners' and 'poulters'.

London Metropolitan Archives contains, apparently, 31 miles of archives, and is the largest local authority record office in the UK. (For further information see p. 49.)

Corporation of London Records Office is available from a link at the very bottom of the homepage. If you're concerned that you are about to be directed back to the Corporation of London website (which, with marvellous illogicality, is at www.cityoflondon.gov.uk, and is described, with all its limitations on p. 117) don't worry; mercifully, this link by-passes that necessity and goes straight to the Records Office itself. Once there, however, beware of clicking on 'Home' at the bottom of any page within this site, or you will indeed find yourself once again doomed to the confusing corridors of the Corporation. Instead, use the blue list at the bottom of the homepage, which begins with Archives and contains such other data as Records of Hospitals, Coroner's Inquests and School Records, and each time you need to return there click 'back' in your top toolbar rather than 'Home' below the list. Downloadable documents, last in the list, will need an Adobe Acrobat reader (see instructions on p. 22).

If at any point you find ancestors in London, which is likely, you will probably need to consult this site, as well as the Corporation of London Records Office and the London Metropolitan Archives, both accessible as links from this site. Few of the records can actually be read online, but at least you can establish which records might be of importance to you, and where they are.

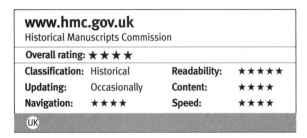

www.hmc.gov.uk
Historical Manuscripts Commission

Overall rating: ★ ★ ★ ★			
Classification:	Historical	**Readability:**	★ ★ ★ ★ ★
Updating:	Occasionally	**Content:**	★ ★ ★ ★
Navigation:	★ ★ ★ ★	**Speed:**	★ ★ ★ ★

UK

The National Register of Archives (NRA) was created by the Commission in 1945 to assemble and make available information about British history source material outside that which is in public records. It has nearly 200,000 lists of manuscript collections, ranging from those in private hands to special holdings in libraries, museums and local record offices, and can normally advise whether such papers are available for research. ARCHON is the information 'gateway' whereby archivists lodge the details of their holdings with the Commission.

SPECIAL FEATURES

Information Sheets (currently 15) are lists of sources to consult on such topics as Business History, History of the Press, History of Education, Colonial History and so on. Testing by looking at 'Sources for Garden History', for instance, brought up an excellent list of relevant organisations to contact, with useful brief details of what the function of each is, as well as a brief bibliography.

Advisory Services offers a limited amount of advice to researchers about accessing records, as well as advice to custodians about the care and preservation of documents.

Manorial Documents Register Use this link to find out which documents are available online (Wales and parts of England).

Publications offers a vast number of reports and calendars, as well as books. It also links to:

Electronic Publications, which can be consulted online, but these are reports on archives and repositories rather than the actual documents they contain. What's New allows you to check progress towards making more documents available online.

A clear, unfussy website probably of most use to those whose research is already fairly advanced and who are starting to explore somewhat more obscure resources.

www.cityoflondon.gov.uk
Corporation of London

Overall rating: ★ ★ ★			
Classification:	Images	**Readability:**	★ ★
Updating:	Occasionally	**Content:**	★ ★ ★ ★
Navigation:	★	**Speed:**	★ ★

UK

Guildhall Library The route to the Library is so tortuous and unsatisfactory that it is far better to enter a new website address altogether, using ihr.sas.ac.uk/gh (see p. 115).

For the genealogist the only real value of this site will be the chance to explore the images gallery under COLLAGE – and that justifies its inclusion here.

The first confusing thing is that the website chooses to carry the title Corporation of London, despite its URL. Then, even if you know that the City of London has an extremely useful library – the Guildhall Library – you look in vain for any mention of it on this homepage. (Don't worry; it has its own website, see p. 115). Before quitting this website, though, take a chance on the COLLAGE image database under Quick Links in the left-hand column.

SPECIAL FEATURES

COLLAGE takes you to the database of the images in the Corporation's collection of paintings, drawings, maps, engravings and photographs. (The name stands for Corporation of London Library and Art Gallery Electronic – logical but remarkably impenetrable until you know!) Many of the images can be ordered online as prints, which can then be posted to you. To find any that might be of relevance to your own search, click on the purple lettering that takes you to the Collage site. You are then offered a search box. Tested with a single, admittedly unusual, surname known to have London associations, this produced three fascinating engravings that were absolutely relevant and previously unknown – a most rewarding result. Below the search box is a generous index of links under topic headings, first in illustrated boxes and, below that, in text. Much time can be happily spent viewing images....

OTHER SITES OF INTEREST

There is not room in this book to list all the good university libraries, let alone all the local libraries that have interesting collections. Many do have websites, however, which can either be accessed from other websites listed here, such as Familia, or by using a general search engine.

John Rylands University of Manchester Methodist Archives and Research Centre
http://rylibweb.man.ac.uk//data1/dg/text/method.html

Genealogy.com
www.genealogy.com
A good US-based library website.
(see p. 39)

Society of Genealogists
www.sog.org.uk
(see p. 36)

Useful addresses

The British Library
96 Euston Road
London
NW1 2DB
tel: *020 7412 7000*

The Earl Consortium for Public Library Networking
Fourth Floor
Gun Court
70 Wapping Lane
London
tel: *020 7702 2020*
fax: *020 7702 2019*

Guildhall Library
Aldermanbury
London
EC2 2EJ
tel: *manuscript section 020 7332 1863*
email: *manuscripts.guildhall@corpoflondon.gov.uk*
              maps and prints 020 7332 1839
              printed books 020 7332 1868/1870
email: *printedbooks.guildhall@corpoflondon.gov.uk*
              bookshop 020 7332 1858
fax: *020 7600 3384*

Historical Manuscripts Commission
Quality House
Quality Court
Chancery Lane
London
WC2A 1HP
tel: *020 7242 1198*
fax: *020 7831 3550*
email: *nra@hmc.gov.uk*

Corporation of London Library and Art Gallery (COLLAGE)
PO Box 270
Guildhall
London
EC2P 2EJ
tel: *020 7606 3030*
email: *pro@corpoflondon.gov.uk*

Society of Genealogists
14 Charterhouse Buildings
Goswell Road
London
EC1M 7BA
tel: 020 7251 8799
fax: 020 7250 1800

Chapter 9

accessories

Most users will probably be familiar already with Amazon.co.uk, bol.co.uk (Books on Line) and other popular book ordering web sites. For the purposes of this Guide, therefore, it seems more relevant to direct users to sources of genealogy books. Jodenoy, listed here, is a particularly good starting point as it has links to several other relevant booksellers. If you want to get an idea of how huge the total range of possibilities is, try using a good search engine such as www.Google.co.uk and entering a request such as

'genealogy bookshops in UK'; doing this has just produced a list of over 300 results, though admittedly one of the first proved to be in Australia!

Having said that, don't necessarily be put off by the thought of ordering from abroad. There is currently no VAT charged on books and carriage costs can be surprisingly reasonable, especially if you are not in a hurry and can opt for surface mail in the case of heavy items. Lighter books travel quickly

Books and Software

and inexpensively anyway. Certainly, if the book you want is rare due to a small print-run, out of print or difficult to find, it may be worth paying to obtain it from abroad.

In the case of second-hand or antiquarian books, again it may be worth looking overseas. For example, a rare history of an English county that would be extremely relevant (and consequently expensive) if sold at home might be languishing on the shelves of a bookseller abroad, under-appreciated and under-priced.

The choice of what software to use for storing your own family history data is a subjective one, so the inclusion here of just two programs, Brother's Keeper and Family Tree Maker, is somewhat arbitrary. Other websites featured here, however, will allow you to compare many different applications.

Two online suppliers of microfiche readers and related products are then detailed, followed by a list of specialists in the restoration of old photographs. Finally, the magazines and journals listed here can all be read either completely or partially online.

www.familytreemaker.com/ftmvers.html
Family Tree Maker

Overall rating: ★ ★ ★ ★			
Classification:	Software	**Readability:**	★ ★ ★ ★ ★
Updating:	Regularly	**Content:**	★ ★ ★ ★
Navigation:	★ ★ ★ ★	**Speed:**	★ ★ ★ ★

US

As the introduction says, this is America's number one selling family tree program. At the time of writing, the newest update is called Version 7.5, the special new feature of which is a 'drag and drop' facility that lets you move or add individual boxes, entire branches or pictures without the need to rearrange the tree as a whole.

SPECIAL FEATURES

Scroll down the homepage to See Family Tree Maker's Awards and Reviews! This should be enough to convince you that FTM is both user-friendly and infinitely expandable (to produce a family tree of up to 99 generations, containing up to 2 million individuals and covering an area 13 miles by 13 miles, if you insist).

Listed below this is an index of features that is initially bewildering. It may help to know that the online records you can consult are listed first; the design features of the FTM software program, in terms of how efficiently it will store your own personal data, are found about halfway down the list; and towards the bottom are the methods whereby you can then share your information with the wider genealogical community.

Once your record-keeping becomes really sophisticated, you may want to explore Genelines in the Genealogy Mall.

To access this, click on the words FamilyTreeMaker.com at the very top of the page you are on, whereupon you will move to the homepage for the FTM website as a whole (see further details on p. 38). At the extreme bottom right corner of this page, click on Turbo-Charged Timelines to learn how you could now place your personal family within a wider historical context.

Incredibly sophisticated, yet by all accounts exceptionally easy to use, Family Tree Maker is state-of-the-art when it comes to organising your own family history records.

www.genfair.com
GENfair

Overall rating: ★ ★ ★ ★			
Classification:	Ecommerce	**Readability:**	★ ★ ★ ★
Updating:	Daily	**Content:**	★ ★ ★ ★
Navigation:	★ ★ ★ ★ ★	**Speed:**	★ ★ ★ ★ ★

UK

Laid out so that users can approach it as if visiting a trade fair, this website contains a wide range of products for purchase that may help the family historian. Click on the GENfair button at the bottom of the page to enter.

SPECIAL FEATURES

Main Hall indexes all the stands, with a particularly good list of Family History Societies, every one with a link to its online presence. Other useful websites are assembled under the title Ancestry Arcade.

GENfair Guide introduces new items for sale, or stands that are newcomers to GENfair, as well as the complete classified list.

Reading Room contains only half a dozen online articles but is still worth a look. One explains calendar changes since 1752, another the etiquette for reimbursing correspondents for their replies, and a third the importance of examining manorial leases.

Location Finder allows you to click on a map of the UK or Ireland (no contributors from the latter yet) and find a list of Family History Societies county by county.

There is, puzzlingly, no link to 'Shop' or some such similar area. Trial and error reveals that in order to start buying you have to click on Classified List and keep working through the various levels (first the stand you want to visit, then a list of what it has for sale) until you finally click on the name of an actual product you wish to purchase. When the name of the item accompanied by a 'basket' logo (sometimes very small) appears, you can click to select that item, whereupon the GENfair: Shopping Basket Review will finally appear. From that point on, instructions are clear.

GENfair Club is promised soon, but had not yet opened when we visited.

As they themselves say, a one-stop shop for all your genealogy needs.

www.genealogy.demon.co.uk
S & N Genealogy

Overall rating: ★ ★ ★ ★			
Classification:	Ecommerce	**Readability:**	★ ★ ★ ★
Updating:	Daily	**Content:**	★ ★ ★ ★
Navigation:	★ ★ ★ ★ ★	**Speed:**	★ ★ ★ ★

UK

A genealogy web site providing computers, computer software, scanners, books, charts and CD data disks. Moreover, S & N offer ongoing support to their customers, without charging premium telephone rates.

They also run training courses for users of Family Tree Maker and Generations Grande Suite, which you can make use of if you can get to Salisbury, where they're based.

SPECIAL FEATURES

Why Buy from S & N? with its link to Customer Comments should convince you of the effieciency of the service.

Genealogy Events is a convenient shortcut to finding out if there are any forthcoming events in your area.

Genealogy Books and Aids offers a useful list of books and booklets as well as, at the bottom of that page, The Ancestral Oak, an attractive chart on which to present six generations of your family tree.

OTHER FEATURES

An alternative method of presentation is found right at the bottom of the homepage, under Other Links. **Your Family Tree with Photographs Web Site** is a link to AncesTree@aol.com, where you can arrange to have up to five generations with photographs mounted on a walnut plaque. This service, you may not be surprised to know, is American.

Essential port-of-call if you need to order computer hardware, software or accessories for genealogy purposes.

www.bkwin.com			
Brother's Keeper			
Overall rating: ★ ★ ★ ★			
Classification: Software		**Readability:**	★ ★ ★ ★
Updating: Weekly		**Content:**	★ ★ ★ ★
Navigation: ★ ★ ★		**Speed:**	★ ★ ★ ★
US			

www.hawgood.co.uk			
David Hawgood			
Overall rating: ★ ★ ★ ★			
Classification: Books		**Readability:**	★ ★ ★ ★
Updating: Weekly		**Content:**	★ ★ ★ ★
Navigation: ★ ★ ★ ★		**Speed:**	★ ★ ★ ★ ★
UK			

Widely respected as one of the best software applications for storing your family history data, Brother's Keeper can be accessed and viewed here online. You can't download the entire program without paying but the chance to have a good look at its capabilities before committing yourself is useful.

The site can also be found at ourworld.compuserve.com/homepages/Brothers_Keeper.

SPECIAL FEATURES

Features include several different ways of presenting your family tree, with pictures or not as you choose. Actual illustrated examples of several of these are shown under sample reports.

The implication of the 'blurb' is that you can 'try out' BK online, whereas what you can actually do is view it, rather than use it. Even that is useful, however.

David Hawgood, sometimes in conjunction with Peter Christian, has written a number of small books about genealogy on the internet.

SPECIAL FEATURES

The main object here is to introduce the various titles by David Hawgood that are currently in print. His most recent title, GENUKI – UK & Ireland Genealogy on the Internet, is available from the homepage in an online form and is a very clear and helpful guide to negotiating the vast resources that GENUKI (see p. 34) contains.

Description of Websites for Finding Surnames on the Hawgood homepage links to all the principal UK genealogical web sites. There are also links to Deja news (see p. 142) and to the Messear system at www.sdtek.com/messear/messear.htm, a service to which you can subscribe and which sifts other lists, emailing you if any new information is posted that relates to your specific surname interests.

There is some good, concise help available here for anyone fairly new to undertaking genealogical research on the internet.

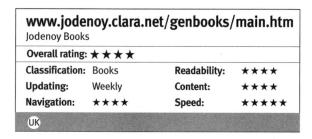

www.jodenoy.clara.net/genbooks/main.htm
Jodenoy Books

Overall rating: ★ ★ ★ ★			
Classification: Books		**Readability:**	★ ★ ★ ★
Updating: Weekly		**Content:**	★ ★ ★ ★
Navigation: ★ ★ ★ ★		**Speed:**	★ ★ ★ ★ ★

UK

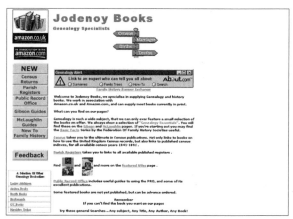

Linked to Amazon.co.uk and Amazon.com, through whom any actual ordering is done, Jodenoy Books, run by Denise Oyston, specialises in genealogy titles in print.

SPECIAL FEATURES

Books are sorted according to the following links: Census Records, Parish Registers, Public Record Office, Gibson Guides, McLaughlin Guides and New to Family History. If Gibson and McLaughlin are unfamiliar names to you, the best route to seeing what these guides cover is to click on their links in the homepage index box, which will give a category list before you start consulting individual titles.

Below the brown index links is a yellow box offering the names of other genealogy booksellers, to which links are also available. On the occasion tested two of these websites were unavailable, one of them being **Booth Books**, which is the link to the book 'town' of Hay-on-Wye. Another book town has now been established in Galloway in Scotland, and the link to that is **GC Books**.

Lesley Aitchison specialises in maps, documents and ephemera, while **Ambra Books** deals with antiquarian and secondhand books relating to Gloucestershire, Wiltshire and counties west. **Stuart Raymond** is another general genealogy specialist selling in-print books.

Incidentally, well towards the bottom of the Jodenoy homepage is a search box linked to Amazon.co.uk where you can try to locate a book via keywords rather than the full title.

This is an excellent route to sifting out genealogy titles, and online ordering is straightforward.

www.mmpublications.co.uk			
MM Publications			
Overall rating: ★ ★ ★ ★			
Classification:	Books	**Readability:**	★ ★ ★ ★ ★
Updating:	Regularly	**Content:**	★ ★ ★ ★ ★
Navigation:	★ ★ ★ ★	**Speed:**	★ ★ ★ ★ ★
UK			

This is the website of Michael McEvoy, specialist in providing British directories in microfiche form. (Incidentally, if the name Ray Sarfas in blue in the bottom left corner of the homepage looks familiar, see Ray's own web site, RS Designs, p. 43.)

SPECIAL FEATURES

This clearly laid-out site provides lists of County Indexes (Pigot's, Kelly's and other directories), Military Indexes and a few Overseas Lists, all available in microfiche form. Miscellaneous is a section well worth studying too. A microfiche viewer with 40x magnification is necessary in order to read these but might well be a worthwhile investment if you want to do serious research from home. Many of the directories listed are rare and probably only found in specialist libraries, while on microfiche they mostly cost only a few pounds.

To order, you need to study the lists under the above headings and make notes of the titles that interest you before moving to the Order Form. You then list the titles and order online, paying by credit card.

A very useful, straightforward service for obtaining information that might otherwise involve a considerable journey.

www.twrcomputing.freeserve.co.uk			
TWR Computing			
Overall rating: ★ ★ ★ ★			
Classification:	Software	**Readability:**	★ ★ ★ ★
Updating:	Regularly	**Content:**	★ ★ ★ ★
Navigation:	★ ★ ★ ★	**Speed:**	★ ★ ★ ★ ★
UK			

This is Trevor Rix's Genealogy and Family History software supplies service, which also offers unlimited, ongoing customer support. Computers and computer programs for other applications are sold too, all with a lowest price guarantee.

SPECIAL FEATURES

Family History and Genealogy Software Click here to access a list of products, first of software programs and then of Data CDs. Ordering is by email, payment by credit card.

The Suffolk 1851 Census listed separately, is available in sections. The link is on the homepage immediately under the yellow box.

Binary Arts Puzzles has absolutely nothing to do with genealogy but may be amusing. These are hand-held brainteasers, all selling for under £10.

A reliable and knowledgeable software supplier, open from 8am to 10pm seven days a week!

www.jenlibrary.u-net.com
The Family History Shop and Library

Overall rating: ★ ★ ★			
Classification: Books		Readability:	★ ★ ★ ★
Updating:	Regularly	Content:	★ ★ ★
Navigation:	★ ★ ★	Speed:	★ ★ ★

(UK)

Jenifer Edmonds set up this service in 1992, when she opened a bricks and mortar shop in Norwich. The Local History & Genealogy Library soon followed.

SPECIAL FEATURES

The homepage offers links to either the Shop or the Library Service. There is a good list of titles available from the Shop, including books, microfiches, maps and other articles. The actual Library in Norwich can be used at a rate of £2.00 per hour. Alternatively you can request printouts of documents, at a rate of £2.00 per surname per index and 10p per sheet. You can communicate by post, telephone or email, and commission either research or courier service delivery of BDM certificates.

The research emphasis is on Norfolk and Suffolk but there are other resources here of good general interest.

OTHER SITES OF INTEREST

Genealogy Books
www.genealogy-books.com
This is the US-based web site of Jeannette Holland Austin. Here you can sign up for a free newsletter, order a CD with 50,000 genealogy links, or select from a catalogue of some 5,000 books.

Stuart Raymond's Internet Genealogical Bookshop
www.soft.net.uk/samjraymond/igb.htm

SEE ALSO

Ancestry.com
www.ancestry.com
(see p. 72)

Cyndi's List
www.cyndislist.com
(see p. 29)

Family History Fairs
www.3w.co.uk/familyhistoryfairs
(see p. 142)

Joe's Genealogy 2000
www.zen.co.uk/home/page/news.htm
(see p. 41)

Public Record Office
www.pro.gov.uk
(see p. 35)

Society of Genealogists
www.sos.org.uk
(see p. 36)

Antiquarian Booksellers

The following are all antiquarian or second-hand book dealers. They all use a system either the same as, or similar to, Amazon, so it does not seem necessary to describe the navigation of each website individually.

Abebooks.com
www.abebooks.com

Alibris
www.alibris.com

Bibliofind
www.bibliofind.com

Biblion
www.biblion.co.uk

Blackwell's Rare Books
http://rarebooks.blackwell.co.uk

Book Avenue
www.bookavenue.com

Ambra Books
www.localhistory.co.uk/ambra

Used Books
www.usedbooks.com

Add ALL
www.addall.com
This site is an umbrella search facility that will sift through many of the above sites

World Book Dealers
www.worldbookdealers.com
A portal for a number of smaller antiquarian and second-

hand dealers, all grouped under this one umbrella.

Amazon

www.amazon.com and www.amazon.co.uk

Both of the Amazon sites have in-print and older books under a specialist genealogy heading.

Roy Davids Ltd

www.rldavids.force9.co.uk

Specialist dealer in manuscripts, letters, archives and portraits, a dangerously enticing place in which to look for that very special present!

Paper Antiques

www.paperantiques.co.uk/dealerspages.htm

An umbrella for a number of dealers in collectibles, ephemera and all sorts of paper memorabilia, including photographs, postcards and cigarette cards.

Reynolds Collectors World

www.reynolds-s-a.freeserve.co.uk/REYNOLDS-COLLECTORS -WORLD/index/html

Specialises in early postcards and other ephemera.

John Townsend

http://freespace.virgin.net/john.townsend2/index.html

John Townsend is an antiquarian bookseller specialising in Genealogy, British Topography and Local History.

Kingfisher Books

www.argonet.co.uk/users/malc.kbs

Kingfisher books will undertake a free book-search for you, and provides a message board where you can post details of books you are seeking on a 'Wants List'.

Magazines and Journals

www.family-tree.co.uk
Family Tree Magazine

Overall rating: ★ ★ ★ ★			
Classification:	Journal	**Readability:**	★ ★ ★ ★ ★
Updating:	Irregularly	**Contents:**	★ ★ ★ ★
Navigation:	★ ★ ★ ★ ★	**Speed:**	★ ★ ★ ★

UK

In its own words, 'the world's best selling British-interest family history journal'.

SPECIAL FEATURES

Contents is located in the top-of-page tabs, and gives a good introduction to what you can expect from any issue of the magazine. The other tabs all have drop-down sub-headings that appear as you put the cursor over each tab. To access the sub-heading you want, you have to click accurately on the relevant word/s, changing the white lettering to a colour (yellow, then red).

Articles lists those articles that appear in the current issue, with a brief synopsis of each. To obtain the Magazine, go to Subscriptions.

Classified explains advertising rates.

PFH introduces 'Practical Family History', the sister publication that is directed to a slightly less knowledgeable readership.

Family Tree Resources allows you to interrogate back issues of the magazine, at which point you may want to go to Online Shop (first in the list of tabs), to buy either a specified back issue or something from their very large and very useful list of books.

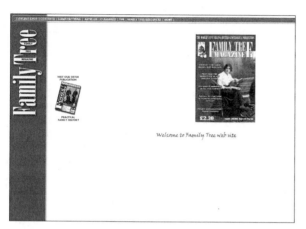

This website will give you a good introduction to what is, without doubt, the best family history magazine for UK users. The Online Shop is well stocked and will no doubt be well used.

www.eurohistory.com/bookstore.htm

European Royal History Bookstore

Overall rating: ★ ★ ★ ★			
Classification:	Bookstore	**Readability:**	★ ★ ★ ★ ★
Updating:	Monthly	**Content:**	★ ★ ★
Navigation:	★ ★ ★ ★	**Speed:**	★ ★ ★ ★
UK			

This is part of the website of European Royal History, dedicated to the publication of a journal about the royal houses of Europe, to which you can subscribe, as well as a large number of articles that can be read online. The Bookstore, selling books both old and new, is well presented, and postcards, some of great historic value, are also either sold directly or at auction.

SPECIAL FEATURES

Links brings up a wonderfully eclectic list of other websites, from the International Romanov Society to Odin's Castle (see p. 114) and Geraldine's Daily Royal News.

About Us introduces, with a photograph, the mastermind behind the site, Arturo E. Beéche.

Sooner or later so many family trees link, however remotely, to a royal line. In that case, this is a good site to explore.

www.everton.com
Everton's Genealogical Helper Magazine

Overall rating: ★ ★ ★			
Classification: Magazine		**Readability:**	★ ★ ★
Updating: n/a		**Contents:**	★ ★ ★
Navigation: ★ ★ ★		**Speed:**	★ ★ ★
US			

magazine and would also allow you to decide whether, rather than becoming a regular subscriber, you should buy a particular issue if it happened to address a topic you wanted to study. The magazine in hard-copy form is available in some UK bookshops.

Certainly a website to look at from time to time, principally to see if any of the current articles address topics of special interest.

This is the online presence of one of the oldest established genealogy magazines, Everton's Genealogical Helper, founded in 1947. Typical of US websites, the pages are busy and bitty, but a lot of information is there if you hunt for it.

SPECIAL FEATURES

Genealogy Reference, near the middle of the links along the top of the homepage, is one of the most helpful. The On-Line Classes are particularly clear, if somewhat chatty in style, and could be very useful to someone exploring the genealogy world for the first time.

Genealogy Supply Store leads to an impressive list, starting with Books but also including such items as CD-ROMs, Magnifiers, Maps and Software. Investigating British Books produced only five titles, however, of which the first was listed as 'A Genealogical Gazateer (sic) of Scotland' so this proved a good deal less helpful than it looked.

Genealogy Magazine Clicking here, second in the top bar, and then on This Issue in the box to the left of the front cover picture, enables you to consult the list of articles in the current issue. You can read the first paragraph or two but not actually read any particular article in its entirety online, because Everton's want you to subscribe, of course. Consulting the list of articles, however, will give you a good idea of the strongly North American emphasis of the

www.onlinegenealogy.com
Journal of Online Genealogy

Overall rating: ★ ★ ★			
Classification:	Journal	**Readability:**	★ ★ ★ ★
Updating:	Regularly	**Contents:**	★ ★ ★
Navigation:	★ ★ ★	**Speed:**	★ ★ ★ ★
US			

This is the website of one of the foremost genealogy periodicals, with articles available for reading online. It is written/edited by April and Matthew Leigh Helm and is presented in a fairly low-key manner, with an index down the left margin and green (unusual colour) links. For unexplained reasons there is a broad blank white column down the right-hand side of each page. On the occasions visited, the text of the lead article ran into this, a layout oddly disturbing to the reader, though subsequent articles were correctly contained.

SPECIAL FEATURES

Internet Gallery, on the right-hand side of the homepage, contains Genealogy Home Page What's Really New, which claims to be the oldest comprehensive genealogy site on the web and apparently listing recently opened internet sites. However, this page was unavailable on the occasions visited.

Genealogy's Most Wanted is a contact forum for researchers, putting them in touch via email or postal addresses. In its first year it received 12,200 listings, from which 96 people found a 'most wanted' person, and several of those stories are told, some rather heart-warming.

Family Finder winks on every page, offering the opportunity to search 275 million names. Clicking transports the user

immediately to FamilyTreeMaker.com (see p. 38), where the name total is apparently 470 million; nevertheless, the list of names is largely dependent on those private individuals who have contributed them. Also, no sum total of results is given as the result of any search, so there is no indication of whether there are a few pages or hundreds to scroll through – a common fault.

Family Toolbox is offered in links down the left-hand, green column. It contains a suite of seven sites designed to help genealogists in their searches, including a list of over 70,000 internet resources, news, reviews, a guide to software, pages for queries and a bookstore.

Helm's Genealogy Toolbox at Genealogy.com (see p. 39) is one of these resources and advertises the forthcoming 'Helm's Genealogy Toolbox Digisources', which will make digitised primary records available online, starting with the complete US Federal Census of 1790.

Again very much aimed at the US user, the links from this site may be of relatively limited use to UK researchers trying to hunt down ancestors. The articles from the Journal of Online Genealogy, however, could be most useful.

www.hmso.gov.uk
Her Majesty's Stationery Office

Overall rating: ★ ★ ★			
Classification:	Magazine	Readability:	★ ★ ★
Updating:	Regularly	Contents:	★ ★ ★ ★
Navigation:	★ ★	Speed:	★ ★ ★

UK

HMSO has printing and editorial responsibilities for Acts of Parliament, Church of England Measures and other Statutory publications.

SPECIAL FEATURES
Most relevant for genealogists and historical researchers is The London Gazette (link available from the homepage), the oldest continuously published newspaper in the UK, founded in 1665. So far, however, only the most recent issues are available for reading online.

Though featuring in most lists of websites of relevance to genealogists, this one seems to have little direct application at present, hence its low overall star-rating here. If early issues of The London Gazette become available online, however, it would be of greater interest.

OTHER SITES OF INTEREST

Eastman's Online Genealogy Newsletter
www.ancestry.com/columns/eastman/index.htm
Click on View the List Archive to bring up a list of recent issues of this American magazine and then click on any particular one to view its contents. The author is Dick Eastman and you can either continue to read the magazine online in future or opt to have it delivered to you by email each week.

Heritage Quest Magazine
www.heritagequest.com
Heritage Quest Newsletter, available by email, and Heritage Quest Magazine, available by subscription, are part of the huge Sierra empire, and are very American in the range of topics they address.

Society of Genealogists
www.sog.org.uk
You can find details of Genealogists' Magazine and Computers in Genealogy, at the website of the Society of Genealogists (see p. 36).

Ancestry.com
www.ancestry.com
Details available of the Product Watch newsletter (see p. 72).

Microfiche Readers

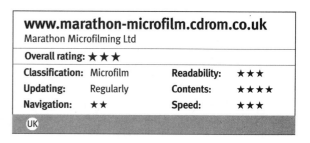

www.marathon-microfilm.cdrom.co.uk
Marathon Microfilming Ltd

Overall rating: ★★★			
Classification:	Microfilm	**Readability:**	★★★
Updating:	Regularly	**Contents:**	★★★★
Navigation:	★★	**Speed:**	★★★

UK

The Marathon Microfilming homepage is reasonably quick to load, but note that About Us is probably off-page until you scroll down using the left-hand index bar. In addition to microfiche readers, Marathon also offer scanning and CD duplication services.

This business does not list prices online, presumably because they change regularly , so you have to telephone or email to obtain price lists.

If you are going to pursue your home-based researches in detail, you will almost certainly need a microfiche reader eventually, and this is a reliable supplier.

www.mw-microfilm.co.uk			
MW Microfilm Supplies			
Overall rating: ★ ★ ★			
Classification: Microfilm		**Readability:**	★ ★ ★
Updating: Occasionally		**Contents:**	★ ★ ★ ★
Navigation: ★ ★		**Speed:**	★ ★ ★
UK			

Photograph Restoration

The rather elaborate homepage of MW Microfilm Supplies is slow to load and the links are not immediately evident, as they merely light up along the bottom of the page when you click on them. They are among the principal suppliers to Genealogists for fiche readers, lamps, binders and other accessories.

As with Marathon Microfilming, they do not list prices online, so again you have to telephone or email for price lists.

Another reliable supplier of microfiche materials.

The first four websites below specialise in the restoration (and sometimes the re-imaging) of old, damaged or torn photographs. All are based in the UK. The fifth, Frank Gavin, is based in Dublin.

Elastic Image
www.elastic-image.co.uk

Kings Vale
http://users.netmatters.co.uk/kingsvale/Home.html

Picture This
www.p-t-r.co.uk

Old Photos Restored, Peter Gibson
www.ambernet.co.uk/old-photos-copied

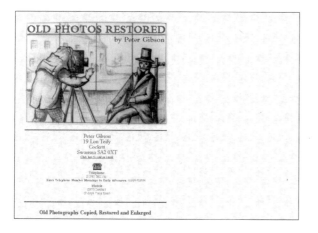

Frank Gavin Photography
www.iol.ie/bizpark/f/franny/index.html

Epson
www.dcs.napier.ac.uk/recall/mm/ColorTutorial_2/CG_HTML/01/010503.HTM
This may seem an an excessively long address, but all of it proves to be necessary, if you wish to view a guide (Epson led) on how to adjust the settings on your scanner, or to use software such as Adobe Photoshop to edit and improve the quality of photographs. Clicking on Home within this website will take you to a more generalised Epson tutorial.

Chapter 10

useful contemporary resources

The services listed here may be of great help to genealogical researchers, even though they are not necessarily designed with such users in mind. Family History Fairs, the first entry, is the one exception. Obviously aimed at genealogists and family historians, the site is listed here because it is mainly devoted to giving details of forthcoming events.

Deja News is featured because you do not need to download a newsreader to access its material and because it is a shortcut to articles from a whole range of newspapers and other publications, thus saving the researcher the need to interrogate newspaper websites individually.

The remaining entries are facilities for tracing missing persons, and online maps for locating places geographically. When searching for missing persons, do be aware that there are some unscrupulous, so-called researchers out there waiting to exploit people in need. The sites listed are reliable.

www.3w.co.uk/familyhistoryfairs
Family History Fairs

Overall rating: ★ ★ ★ ★			
Classification:	Events	**Readability:**	★ ★ ★ ★
Updating:	Regularly	**Content:**	★ ★ ★ ★
Navigation:	★ ★ ★	**Speed:**	★ ★ ★

UK

www.deja.com/usenet
Deja.com

Overall rating: ★ ★ ★ ★			
Classification:	News	**Readability:**	★ ★ ★ ★
Updating:	Regularly	**Content:**	★ ★ ★
Navigation:	★ ★ ★	**Speed:**	★ ★ ★ ★

US

In addition to a simple list of forthcoming events, there is a short but useful index two-thirds of the way down the homepage of stall holders' websites.

This is a news search-engine service, totally contemporary and up-to-date in its intentions, so not at first sight apparently all that relevant to genealogists. Think again!

SPECIAL FEATURES

Click Here for Event Dates Click here first to get at the current listing, and then on Click Here for Latest Dates.

A visit to a Family History Fair can be most helpful, especially as it gives you the chance to pick the brains of other genealogy enthusiasts, as well as see products such as books, magazines and software at first hand.

This is the shortcut to discovering when the next Family History Fair will be in your area. There are some worthwhile additional links to be found at the websites of individual stall holders.

SPECIAL FEATURES

Simply use the 'search' box to test whether there has been anything recently published, including messages posted online, on whatever topic interests you. For example, the word 'genealogy' immediately produced more than 4,500 'hits'; admittedly, some had been entered several times, and some group entries from the same article had been posted on the same date, so refining the search was clearly necessary. The system works, though. On the occasion tested, two vaguely remembered articles on fairly obscure topics were immediately found, despite the scantiest of information.

Only articles of relatively recent date are available, so this cannot be used as, for instance, an obituary search.

If you seem to remember having seen a recent article about a topic that interests you and can't remember where, this is a good place to look.

www.teldir.com
Telephone Directories on the Web

Overall rating: ★ ★ ★ ★

Classification:	Contacts	Readability:	★ ★ ★ ★ ★
Updating:	Regularly	Content:	★ ★ ★ ★ ★
Navigation:	★ ★ ★ ★	Speed:	★ ★ ★ ★

INT

Indispensable tool for tracking down living contacts worldwide, even though some countries are not yet fully listed. For instance, a test for a South African number revealed that only business numbers are so far listed there, not personal numbers. Both types of number are available for the UK and the US, however.

SPECIAL FEATURES

Email Addresses, bottom left-hand box on the homepage, links to several directories, although none of them is very complete, and there are certainly many obsolete addresses, as the online reviewer points out.

Frequently Asked Questions explains the position on things like fax numbers, unsolicited contacts and privacy issues.

CallNOW.com is where you can sign up to save money on international calls, the system being that you connect briefly, hang up and wait to be called back immediately by the CallNow network, and then you redial.

First-stop location for finding the telephone numbers of living people or existing businesses.

www.uksearches.com
UK Electoral Roll Searches

Overall rating: ★ ★ ★ ★

Classification:	Records	Readability:	★ ★ ★ ★
Updating:	Regularly	Content:	n/a
Navigation:	★ ★ ★ ★	Speed:	★ ★ ★ ★

UK

This is a fee-paying tracing service claiming a very high record of success.

SPECIAL FEATURES

Information Choosing from the links in the left-hand margin, click here to discover why Helen Rowland set up this service, and then on Services and Contact Us for further information. Services are not available to anyone under the age of 18. Contact is by telephone (preferred), fax or email, and the standard fee (currently £15) is not charged if the search is unsuccessful. Initial approaches will be made on your behalf, if required, in the case of adoptees or foster children trying to find birth parents, or for those trying to re-establish contact with friends or relatives after some sort of rift.

Hyperlinks brings up a useful list of other organisations, such as The Police and The Samaritans, who may be able to help.

Bulletin leads to a free message board service, but the messages are posted simply in the order received, so the chances of a successful outcome by this method seem less likely.

If you are prepared to pay for a result, this would seem to be an excellent place to start your search for anyone, from a long-lost relative to a school-friend, with whom you simply happen to have lost touch.

www.lookupuk.com
Lookup United Kingdom

Overall rating: ★ ★ ★			
Classification:	Records	**Readability:**	★ ★ ★ ★
Updating:	Occasionally	**Content:**	★ ★
Navigation:	★ ★ ★	**Speed:**	★ ★

UK

www.multimap.com
Multimap.com

Overall rating: ★ ★ ★			
Classification:	Records	**Readability:**	★ ★ ★
Updating:	Occasionally	**Content:**	★ ★ ★ ★
Navigation:	★ ★ ★	**Speed:**	★ ★ ★

UK

Slow to load, as they warn you on the homepage, this website claims to be the largest service in the UK for finding missing persons.

SPECIAL FEATURES

The site is divided into three: Adoption Related, non-Adoption Related and Genealogy Related, the last of which is again divided, by country, into England, Scotland, Ireland (including Northern Ireland) and Wales. Instructions are clear, though you may wonder who takes the time to read through all the already posted messages, especially since they are in no particular order but are just listed by date of receipt, most recent first. Also, it is not clear whether there is any system for removing messages, either when successfully answered or simply after time. Movement around the site is certainly slow.

Other UK Resources, in the left-of-page index, has a brief list of UK Genealogy Links, one of which goes to GenDex, where among other things you can rent storage space for your family history files.

This will be of limited use, but tracing living relatives will remain a problem until a more efficient way of doing it is developed.

Subtitled 'A Complete Interactive Atlas on the Web', this is, in effect, an online gazetteer.

SPECIAL FEATURES

If you need to find where a particular parish or hamlet is, simply input either the name or the postcode (with no gaps between letters/numbers), and use Search to produce a map. To enlarge the scale, alter the scale figure, moving to a lower number; to reduce, do the reverse.

Local Websites Clicking here will then produce a list of options, including Pubs, Restaurants, Hotels and Local Info Sites, any of which might be very useful if you need to visit an area you do not know.

Useful as a shortcut to locating any British placename. The onward links, in terms of local information, were not by any means all working on the occasion tested.

www.missing-you.net
Missing You

Overall rating: ★ ★			
Classification:	Records	**Readability:**	★ ★ ★
Updating:	Occasionally	**Content:**	n/a
Navigation:	★ ★	**Speed:**	★ ★

UK

This free online service has been associated with the BBC's 'The Search' campaign (to which there is a link from the homepage), featured in The Daily Mirror and The Daily Mail, and is sponsored by Peopletracer. You can post a free message in search of a missing person (presumed still alive), giving your email address for a reply, and at the same time search the list of messages posted by others. Until recently, the frustration was that the messages were in no particular order, but simply listed by the date on which they were posted and only sifted according to the region of the country to which they applied, such as south west, north east and so on – and they were becoming very numerous! The introduction of a new Search Engine, found under Search Website in the left-column index, now allows you to specify the name, subject or locality to be found from within the vast bank of messages.

SPECIAL FEATURES

Click on the yellow **Index** button to move from the introductory page to the homepage. Here the index gives good help, first listing all the UK regions and then the various services.

A **Genealogy Messaging Service** is included, but at the time of testing it was suffering from overload and no more messages were being accepted until the existing backlog had been cleared.

Adoptions, not recorded regionally, links to Adoption UK. There is also an Armed Forces link.

QUICKtrace is a specialist online tracing service with additional power and speed costing £20, which, they claim, is probably the lowest of any UK tracing service (see UK Electoral Roll Searches, on p. 143, though).

There is certainly a need for this sort of missing persons service, especially if the link with the more or less universal medium of television can be used, but it still needs to be much more widely publicised so that more people are aware of its existence. A good idea, though.

OTHER SITES OF INTEREST

GradFinder
www.gradfinder.com

This international service, operating in 69 countries, seeks to put school and college graduates back in touch.

Ordnance Survey
www.ordsvy.gov.uk/getamap/index.html

This offers a similar service to Multimap (see p. 144), where you are permitted to print off maps free of charge, provided they are not for commercial use. However, there are no onward local links of the Multimap kind.

Glossary of Internet Terms

A

Accelerators Add-on programs, which speed up browsing.

Acceptable Use Policy These are the terms and conditions of using the internet. They are usually set by organisations, who wish to regulate an individual's use of the internet. For example, an employer might issue a ruling on the type of email which can be sent from an office.

Access Provider A company which provides access to the internet, usually via a dial-up account. Many companies such as AOL and Dircon charge for this service, although there are an increasing number of free services such as Freeserve, Lineone and Tesco.net. Also known as an Internet Service Provider.

Account A user's internet connection, with an Access/Internet Service Provider, which usually has to be paid for.

Acrobat Reader Small freely-available program, or web browser plug-in, which lets you view a Portable Document Format (PDF) file.

Across Lite Plug-in which allows you to complete crossword puzzles online.

Address Location name for email or internet site, which is the online equivalent of a postal address. It is usually composed of a unique series of words and punctuation, such as *my.name@myhouse.co.uk*. See also URL.

America Online (AOL) World's most heavily subscribed online service provider.

Animated GIF Low-grade animation technique used on websites.

ASCII Stands for American Standard Code for Information Interchange, It is a coding standard which all computers can recognise, and ensures that if a character is entered on one part of the internet, the same character will be seen elsewhere.

ASCII Art Art made of letters and other symbols. Because it is made up of simple text, it can be recognised by different computers.

ASDL Stands for Asynchronous Digital Subscriber Line, which is a high speed copper wire which will allow rapid transfer of information. Not widely in use at moment, though the government is pushing for its early introduction.

Attachment A file included with an email, which may be composed of text, graphics and sound. Attachments are encoded for transfer across the internet, and can be viewed in their original form by the recipient. An attachment is the equivalent of putting a photograph with a letter in the post.

B

Bookmark A function of the Netscape Netvigator browser which allows you to save a link to your favourite web pages, so that you can return straight there at a later date, without having to re-enter the address. Favourites in internet Explorer is the same thing.

BPS Abbreviation of Bits Per Second, which is a measure of the speed at which information is transferred or downloaded.

Browse Common term for looking around the web. See also Surfing.

Browser A generic term for the software that allows users to move and look around the Web. Netscape Navigator and

Internet Explorer are the ones that most people are familiar with, and they account for 97 percent of web hits.

Bulletin Board Service A BBS is a computer with a telephone connection, which allows you direct contact to upload and download information and converse with other users, via the computer. It was the forerunner to the online services and virtual communities of today.

C

Cache A temporary storage space on the hard drive of your computer, which stores downloaded websites. When you return to a website, information is retrieved from the cache and displayed much more rapidly. However, this information may not be the most recent version for sites which are frequently updated and you will need to reload the website address for these.

Chat Talking to other users on the web in real time, but with typed, instead of spoken words. Special software such as ICQ or MIRC is required before you can chat.

Chat Room An internet channel which allows several people to type in their messages, and talk to one another over the internet.

Clickstream The trail left as you 'click' your way around the web.

Content The material on a website that actually relates to the site, and is hopefully of interest or value. Things like adverts are not considered to be part of the content. The term is also used to refer to information on the internet that can be seen by users, as opposed to programming and other background information.

Cookie A cookie is a nugget of information sometimes sent by websites to your hard drive when you visit. They contain such details as what you looked at, what you ordered, and can add more information, so that the website can be customized to suit you.

Cybercafe Cafe where you can use a computer terminal to browse the net for a small fee.

Cyberspace When first coined by the sci-fi author William Gibson, it meant a shared hallucination which occured when people logged on to computer networks. Now, it refers to the virtual space you're in when on the internet.

D

Dial Up A temporary telephone connection to your ISP's computer and how you make contact with your ISP, each time you log onto the internet.

Domain The part of an internet address which identifies an individual computer, and can often be a business or person's name. For example, in the goodwebguide.com the domain name is theGoodWebGuide.

Download Transfer of information from an internet server to your computer.

Dynamic HTML The most recent version of the HTML standard.

E

Ecash Electronic cash, used to make transactions on the internet.

Ecommerce The name for business which is carried out over the internet.

Email Mail which is delivered electronically over the internet. They are usually comprised of text messages, but can contain illustrations, music and animations. Mail is sent to an email address, which is the internet equivalent of a postal address.

Encryption A process whereby information is scrambled to produce a 'coded message', so that it can't be read whilst in transit on the internet. The recipient must have decryption software in order to read the message.

Expire Term referring to newsgroup postings which are automatically deleted after a fixed period of time.

Ezine Publication on the web, which is updated regularly.

F

FAQ Stands for frequently asked questions and is a common section on websites where the most common enquiries and their answers are archived.

Frame A method which splits web pages into several windows.

FTP/File Transfer Protocol Standard method for transporting files across the internet.

G

GIF/Graphics Interchange Format A format in which graphics are compressed, and a popular method of putting images onto the internet, as they take little time to download.

Gopher The gopher was the precursor of the world wide web and consisted of archives accessed through a menu, usually organised by subject.

GUI/Graphical User Interface. This is the system which turns binary information into the words and images format you can see on your computer screen. For example, instead of seeing the computer language which denotes the presence of your toolbar, you actually see a toolbar.

H

Hackers A term used to refer to expert programmers who used their skills to break into computer systems, just for the fun of it. Nowadays the word is more commonly associated with computer criminals, or Crackers.

Header Basic indication of what's in an email: who it's from, when it was sent, and what it's about.

Hit When a file is downloaded from a website it is referred to as a 'hit'. Measuring the number of hits is a rough method of counting how many people visit a website. Except that it's not wholly accurate as one website can contain many files, so one visit by an individual may generate several hits.

Homepage Most usually associated with a personal site, produced by an individual, but can also refer to the first page on your browser, or the first page of a website.

Host Computer on which a website is stored. A host computer may store several websites, and usually has a fast powerful connection to the internet. Also known as a Server.

HTML/Hypertext Mark-Up Language The computer code used to construct web pages.

HTTP/Hypertext Transfer Protocol The protocol for moving HTML files across the web.

Hyperlink A word or graphic formatted so that when you click on it, you move from one area to another. See also hypertext.

Hypertext Text within a document which is formatted so it acts as a link from one page to another, or from one document to another.

I

Image Map A graphic which contains hyperlinks.

Interface What you actually see on the computer screen.

Internet One or more computers connected to one another is an internet (lower case i). The Internet is the biggest of all the internets and consists of a worldwide collection of interconnected computer networks.

Internet Explorer One of the most popular pieces of browser software, produced by Microsoft.

Intranet A network of computers, which works in the same way as an internet, but for internal use, such as within a corporation.

ISDN/Integrated Services Digital Network Digital telephone line which facilitates very fast connections and can transfer larges amounts of data. It can carry more than one form of data at once.

ISP/Internet Service Provider See Access Provider.

J

Java Programming language which can be used to create interactive multimedia effects on webpages. The language is used to create programmes known as *applets* that add features such as animations, sound and even games to websites.

Javascript A scripting language which, like Java, can be used to add extra multimedia features. However, in contrast with Java it does not consist of separate programmes. Javascript is embedded into the HTML text and can interpreted by the browser, provided that the user has a javascript enabled browser.

JPEG Stands for 'Joint Photographic Experts Group' and is the name given to a type of format which compresses photos, so that they can be seen on the web.

K

Kill file A function which allows a user to block incoming information from unwanted sources. Normally used on email and newsreaders.

L

LAN/Local Area Network A type of internet, but limited to a single area, such as an office.

Login The account name or password needed to access a computer system.

Link Connection between web pages, or one web document and another, which are accessed via formatted text and graphic.

M

Mailing List A discussion group which is associated with a website. Participants send their emails to the site, and it is copied and sent by the server to other individuals on the mailing list.

Modem A device for converting digital data into analogue signals for transmission along standard phone lines. The usual way for home users to connect to the internet or log into their email accounts. May be internal (built into the computer) or external (a desk-top box connected to the computer).

MP3 A compressed music file format, which has almost no loss of quality although the compression rate may be very high.

N

Netscape Popular browser, now owned by AOL.

Newbie Term for someone new to the internet. Used perjoratively of newcomers to bulletin boards or chat, who commit the sin of asking obvious questions or failing to observe the netiquette.

Newsgroup Discussion group amongst internet users who share a mutual interest. There are thousands of newsgroups covering every possible subject.

O

Offline Not connected to the internet via a telephone line.

Online Connected to the internet via a telephone line.

Offline Browsing A function of the browser software, which allows the user to download pages and read them whilst offline.

Online Service Provider Similar to an access provider, but provides addtional features such as live chat.

P

PDF/Portable Document Format A file format created by Adobe for offline reading of brochures, reports and other documents with complex graphic design, which can be read by anyone with Acrobat Reader.

Plug-in Piece of software which adds more functions (such as playing music or video) to another, larger software program.

POP3/Post Office Protocol An email protocol that allows you to pick up your mail from any location on the web.

Portal A website which offers many services, such as search engines, email and chat rooms, and to which people are likely to return to often . ISPs such as Yahoo and Alta Vista provide portal sites which are the first thing you see when you log on, and in theory act as gateways to the rest of the web.

Post/Posting Information sent to a usenet group, bulletin board, message board or by email.

PPP/Point to Point Protocol The agreed way of sending data over dial-up connections, so that the user's computer, the modem and the Internet Server can all recognise it. It is the protocol which allows you to get online.

Protocol Convention detailing a set of actions that computers in a network must follow so that they can understand one another.

Q

Query Request for specific information from a database.

R

RAM /Random Access Memory Your computer's short term memory.

Realplayer G2 A plug-in program that allows you to view video in real-time and listen to sound and which is becoming increasingly important for web use.

Router A computer program which acts as an interface between two networks, and decides how to route information.

S

Searchable Database A database on a website which allows the user to search for information, usually be keyword.

Search Engine Programs which enable web users to search for pages and sites using keywords. They are usually to be found on portal sites and browser homepages. Infoseek, Alta Vista and Lycos are some of the popular search engines.

Secure Transactions Information transfers which are encrypted so that only the sender and recipient have access to the uncoded message, so that the details within remain private. The term is most commonly used to refer to credit card transactions, although other information can be sent in a secure form.

Server A powerful computer that has a permanent fast connection to the internet. Such computers are usually owned by companies and act as host computers for websites.

Sign-on To connect to the internet and start using one of its facilities.

Shareware Software that doesn't have to be paid for or test version of software that the user can access for free, as a trial before buying it.

Standard A style which the whole of the computer industry has agreed upon. Industry standards mean that hardware and software produced by the various different computer companies will work with one another.

Surfing Slang for looking around the Internet, without any particular aim, following links from site to site.

T

TLA/Three Letter Acronyms Netspeak for the abbreviations of net jargon, such as BPS (Bits Per Second) and ISP (Internet Service Provider).

U

Upload To send files from your computer to another one on the internet. When you send an email you are uploading a file.

URL/Uniform Resource Locator Jargon for an address on the internet, such as www.thegoodwebguide.co.uk.

Usenet A network of newsgroups, which form a worldwide system, on which anyone can post 'news'.

V

Virtual Community Name given to a congregation of regular mailing list/ newsgroup users.

VRML/Virtual Reality Modeling Language Method for creating 3D environments on the web.

W

Wallpaper Description of the sometimes hectic background patterns which appear behind the text on some websites.

Web Based Email/Webmail Email accounts such as Hotmail and Rocketmail, which are accessed via an internet browser, rather than an email program such as Outlook Express.

Webmail has to be typed whilst the user is online, but can accessed from anywhere on the Web.

Webmaster A person responsible for a web server. May also be known as System Administrator.

Web Page Document which forms one part of a website (though some sites are a single page), usually formatted in HTML.

Web Ring Loose association of websites which are usually dedicated to the same subject and often contain links to one another.

Website A collection of related web pages which often belong to an individual or organisation and are about the same subject.

World Wide Web The part of the internet which is easy to get around and see. The term is often mistakely interchanged with Internet, though the two are not the same. If the Internet is a shopping mall, with shops, depots, and delivery bays, then the web is the actual shops which the customers see and use.

index

How to use your CD

Now we've whetted your appetite for the sites reviewed in this book, we can help you to visit them quickly and easily. By registering on thegoodwebguide site, you will be able to use the hotlinks to all the sites listed, so you just click and go. You can also read the latest versions of reviews and see what we think of new sites that have been launched since the book went to press. If you wish, you can even have the updates emailed to you.

INSTALLATION INSTRUCTIONS FOR PC USERS

Insert the CD enclosed with this book into your CD drive of your PC. A welcome screen will appear with two buttons:

The goodwebguide button To register your purchase of a Good Web Guide book and to receive free updates of the reviews in the book and reviews of the latest sites, click on this button. When you've registered you can click straight through to any of the sites listed. You must have an internet connection to do this. If you are not already signed up with an internet service, you will need to install the LineOne software first.

If you click on the goodwebguide button you will be taken to a registration page where you will be asked to confirm which title in the series you have bought and to register your details. You then have free access to the updates of the website reviews in this book and to new reviews. You will also have access to the rest of the goodwebguide website.

LineOne button If you would like access to the internet you can click on this button to install LineOne's free ISP (internet service provider) software. You will need a modem to have internet access. If you already have an internet connection (ISP) you can still install LineOne as an alternative provider.

A To join LineOne just click on the LineOne button. When the first screen appears you have a choice: If you are a new user and wish to load Internet Explorer 5 as your browser, select 'Join Now'. On the next screen, select 'Go!' and you will be taken to the Microsoft installation process.

B To join immediately, without installing a browser, click 'Join Now' and then choose 'custom' to go straight to registration.

From the 'Welcome to LineOne' screen, click 'Go' and follow the on-screen instructions.

MAC USERS

This CD is not suitable for Apple Macintosh computers. For Free LineOne Mac Software call free on 0800 111 210.

RETURNING TO THE GOOD WEB GUIDE

Once you've connected to the internet, you can either type www.thegoodwebguide.co.uk into your browser to go directly to our website, or re-insert your CD and click on the goodwebguide button.

SUPPORT
If you have any problems call the LineOne support number. **CALL 0906 30 20 100**
(calls may be monitored or recorded for training purposes) 24 hours, 365 days a year. Calls charged at 50p/minute or email support@lineone.net for free support.

Other great titles in thegoodwebguide series:

Money	Gardening	Food	Parents
ISBN 1-903282-02-0	ISBN 1-903282-00-4	ISBN 1-903282-01-2	ISBN 1-903282-03-9

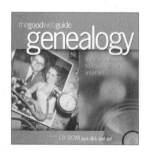

Genealogy	Travel	Wine	Health
ISBN 1-903282-06-3	ISBN 1-903282-05-5	ISBN 1-903282-04-7	ISBN 1-903282-08-X